BROKEN
(Lies, Deception, & Love)

A novel by
D. SHAHID & E.W. Gaskin

About The Author

D. Shahid is a throwback native New Yorker. He is committed to change, rehabilitation, and evolution. D. Shahid is the co-founder of the Heart of a Hustla brand, and Co-Owner of Heart of a H.U.S.T.L.A. Publishing. D. Shahid is dedicated to changing the negative connotations attached to the term Hustla. H.U.S.T.L.A. is an acronym that represents:

H. HAVING

U. UNDYING

S. STRENGTH

T. TO

L. LEVITATE

A. ABOVE

Levitating above any obstacle that life may throw at you is his definition of what a Hustla is. D. Shahid is the epitome of the term H.U.S.T.L.A. He himself has levitated and overcome lifestyle choices that cost him 20 years of his life. He Has Undying Strength to levitate above because he is the true definition of a H.U.S.T.L.A.

Copyright Page

Copyright © 2023 Heart Of A Hustla Publishing LLC.

All rights reserved. No portion of this book may be reproduced in any form without permission from the publisher, except as permitted by U.S. copyright law. For permissions contact: readingisfundamental@heartofahustla.org

Acknowledgments

D.Shahid would like to acknowledge his QUEEN Chevi for all the support and the thought she sparks. He dedicates this book to her. To his Rocks: Jay, Zay, Ken, and Sam. .. The world is yours!

Special thanks to the models Mr. Sadik and Mrs. Kevi Gaskin.
If you are in need of a physical fitness trainer in the Atlanta GA area contact on IG@ohsnapthatssadiq

Thanks to Redesign your life, LLC for the priceless game. If you are in need of a life coach contact Dr. Tandy on IG @lifecoachtandy. I would also like to thank Marie White, CEO of The Brand Boutique. If you need to build a digital brand go to IG @thebrandboutique

To the Gaskin, Dudley, and Palmers..... SALUTE!!!!!

Acknowledgments

ALLAH forgive me for anything Haram & bless me for anything that's Halal.

To my kids, I love you ALL more than u will ever know. There are no FAVORITES, Just unconditional LOVE. Those who have their eyes closed, One day u will see the truth. Stay close to one another and remember u now have a little brother, LOVE HIM.

To My Mom, who played a role of my dad as well. The way u love us was a blessing and I will always know that. Thank you for your love. I HEAR U. They say your sickness is from u not being close to GOD, but in fact it's proof GOD loves you. Jealous ones envy.

To my brother, Thank You for having my back when I needed you. We will never allow anything to divide us. Nothing better than a brother's love. Loyalty, The true cloth of a Gaskin.   THANK U

To my sister, thank you for teaching me to never fear any man. I love you.
To ALL my nieces/nephews plus Grands, I love U guys, always have.

Queen Zebiba You are truly sent from ALLAH Thank u for allowing me to lead you. Thank you for loving me and staying on me about my dean. There's no King without a Queen.

To my Daughter-law, Thank u for loving my son & blessing our book with your beauty. I need to hear from u more. Sadik thank u for always loving me no matter what. Thank you for the respect you have always shown me. Loyalty, Thank you for sharing your presents in BROKEN. You're a beast. The true cloth of a Gaskin. You guys are the better version of Lorna & I. Never quit on each other, see it through.

Samantha, you will always be my daughter and We love you. BE IN OUR LIVES.

To my ride, or die CUZ. If I ever had to go to war, I know you in the front seat. From music and now books (We Back). We finally will show the world our masterpiece. We put our foot in this. Let's show them family can do it. Thank you for being The true cloth of a Gaskin.

Some people are MAD at me because I'm not suffering the way they expected me to. May ALLAH keep on disappointing them.

This book is dedicated to 60% of the women I know, family, friends, and others who have been raped molested, and abused.

Thank you, family, friends, and those who purchase our book.

Yours truly E W Gaskin AKA Never good enough.

CHAPTER 1

As I fade in and out of consciousness, I wonder... How did I get to this point? What wrong turns in my life drove me to being handcuffed to this bed? What choices led me to being drugged by my lover, and now on the brink of death? What decisions pushed me to cheat on my husband Mark? Damn, I have to try and stay awake. The darkness keeps pulling closer though. It seems so peaceful in the dark. It feels like a place void of any drama. *I'm so tired of drama. God knows my life has been drama filled as of late. How did it get to this point? How did I, Dr. Kimberly Stevens, allow myself to go out like this? Oh no! Here comes another wave of darkness.*

Several Years Earlier...

"I'm telling you, Steph, I don't have any time to be clubbing. These classes are killing me. I'm just feeling too swamped right now." The overload of graduate classes was taking its toll on Kim.

"I'm telling you, Kim, you're gonna burn yourself out. Remember that Chinese chick that used to be in our classes? You see what happened to her, right? That poor child fried her damn brain," Stephanie joked. "You need to get out and let loose sometimes, dang! Girl, you be acting like you are somebody's grandma."

Stephanie was Kim's best friend. The two came up together ever since grade school in Queens. Stephanie's mother got caught up in the whole crack epidemic of '86. That caused Stephanie to spend most of her time at Kim's house. The two girls grew as close as blood sisters. In their youth, they made a pact that when they grew up, they would become doctors. The women were now turning that dream into a reality.

"You may be right," Steph chuckled. "I don't want these scrubs all up in my face." Stephanie had to laugh at this. She had witnessed her friend embarrass many men throughout the years. Kim was known to be an assassin to the male's fragile ego.

Kimberly was a fine sister. She stood at 5'7" tall and sported a copper penny complexion. Her hair was styled in a short bob reminiscent of Anita Baker. The track team that she was a member of demanded that she maintain her figure. She was tight, right, and at the same time curvy. That in addition to her intelligence attracted many men. Kim was vibrant, confident, fully focused, and nonsense free. Kimberly's motto was that she had no time for fake ones and she had no time for games. This being the case, she chose to be single and celibate.

"Girrrrl, this music is bumping. This is my jam right here!" Stephanie said as she snapped her fingers to the music. She was determined to facilitate Kim's enjoyment. "It's a'ight," Kim said teasingly. She was also enjoying the scene. The lounge provided a nice vibe with an adult atmosphere. They catered to the so-called "professional" crowd. The truth of the matter was that the professionals partied just as hard as the unprofessional or the uncouth did.

The DJ continued to mix all of the butter jams. Kim couldn't help but be invaded by the pulsating vibrations. Kim's energy was spotted by Mark. Her aura was magnetic and it pulled Mark to Kim. Mark chose not to rush her in an immature nature though. He forewent that strategy and opted to just observe her intermittently. "Kim, a cutie got you in his scopes, girl," Stephanie informed her.

"Where?" Kim asked. She looked in the direction that Stephanie was pointing. Looking back at her, not masking his attraction, was Mark. Their eyes met, but Kim quickly averted them. "He is a cutie," Kim agreed. "Most likely he's probably a player though." Stephanie shook her head pityingly. "You just gonna categorize him like that? You just gonna shut him down? Dang, girl, you ain't even gonna give the brother a shot? Look at that man, Kim. He's fine as hell. Shit, if you don't want him, I'll take him."

Kim wasn't surprised at Stephanie's response. "Do what you feel is real, Steph. I don't have any time for no wannabe playas. I don't do games, love, so like I said, do you. This was typical of Stephanie. When it came to men, she was the complete opposite of Kim. Where Kim was closed, Stephanie was wide open. In Kim's eyes she was too loose, but she loved and accepted her despite their differences. Stephanie's upbringing caused her to be starved.

This shortcoming exposed itself in the relationship department. Due to the absence of her father, she always felt as though she needed the love of a man. Sadly, like many women, Stephanie equated sex with love. This being the case, the initial abandonment of her father was felt each time a relationship ended. Men were in and out of her life routinely. "I'll be right back." Stephanie made her way over to Mark. Mark peeped Stephanie as she seductively approached him.

He was used to females coming onto him regularly. Mark stood 6 feet tall with a muscular build. He had brown paper bag complexioned skin. Mark wasn't compulsive about his appearance, but he kept his grooming up to par. His Caesar was always cut clean, his sideburns and goatee were sculpted perfectly, and his dimples were deep to assure a perfect smile. The swagger and confidence that exuded from Mark were like an aphrodisiac to most women. He prided himself on being a conversationalist. The code that Mark lived by was "conversation rules the nation." "I see you standing here all by yourself, handsome. My name is Stephanie. And yours, boo?" Mark blessed Stephanie with one of his dazzling smiles. "Pleasure to meet you, Stephanie," Mark said, giving her the once over. "My name is Mark. So are you enjoying yourself tonight?"

Stephanie, being her typical self, responded with a sexual innuendo. "I don't know, am I? If you're with it, then I'm with it." Initially Mark was taken aback, but he quickly recovered. Before he could make a suggestive reply, he looked up in time to catch Kimberly watching. Once again, he was tugged by her gravitational forces.

"I'm flattered, Stephanie. I can't front. You, my dear, definitely have it going on." In that regard, Mark wasn't lying. Stephanie was surely a brick house beauty. She stood about 5'10". Stephanie was kissed with a honey gold complexion. Her curves and physique rivaled that of any video vixen. Her green eyes were her best characteristic. He looked directly into her mesmerizing eyes and decided to gamble on Kim.

"But I don't know why, I feel an attraction to your girl over there." Stephanie felt a twinge of dejection, but it was all love between her and Kim. There wasn't any competitive or jealous spirit between the two. "Oh, you're feeling my girl, boo-boo? Well, follow me then, and let introduce you to her." Mark couldn't believe Stephanie. As he followed her, he took another peek at her scrumptious-looking backyard. He thought to himself, *This girl right here is a wild one.* Kimberly saw Steph walking back towards her with the same cutie in tow. "Hey Kim, this is Mark. Mark, this is Kim," Stephanie introduced the pair. "Kim, girl, you ain't gonna believe this.

I tried to get my mack on with Mark, but he talking about 'I feel a connection to your girl over there.' " This caused both ladies to giggle. "So here you are. See if the connection he felt is a love connection. I'm going to the bar to get me a strawberry daiquiri." Stephanie walked off, leaving the two in an awkward silence. This was done in an effort to give them space in order to connect. Kim let out an embarrassed chuckle. " So what type of lame game are you kicking?

Mark laughed and looked at Kim sideways. "Why I got to be lame, and why do I have to be kicking some type of game?" Mark asked. "I'm saying, what is your name again? Mark? You don't know me from Eve and you telling my girl you feel a connection? Come on, bruh, if that's not some see-through lame game, then I don't know what is." Mark feigned a look of being appalled. At that, Kim laughed even harder. "Well first of all, Ms. Kim, think about this for a second, if you will. If I was out and about randomly kicking game with the hopes of having a good time, then I could've just bagged your girl. She was all over me. She gave me all the rhythm."

Kim believed this. She wasn't surprised at Steph. "Second of all, I'm in tune with the universe. It's possible to feel someone's energy without even coming into direct contact with them. And I must say, Ms. Kim, your energy feels so damn good to me."

Once again Kimberly laughed, but not with the authority of dismissal. "Third of all, Ms. Kim, based on that energy, I feel a connection to you. And let me add for the record, I'm far from a lame. Furthermore, I don't have any frivolous time to be out here kicking game. Who you supposed to be anyway, Kim? You ain't the queen bee, Li'l Kim. You're rhyming and shit talking about your see-through lame game. Sounds like you trying to rap. Let me find out you trying to be a rapper." At that, they both burst out laughing. This caused Kim to lower her guards a little. "You wanna know what my daddy says?" Kim asked. Mark nodded an answer. "He says to be careful of the ones that keep you laughing."

That day began the first day of many together. Mark and Kim developed a healthy friendship together. Whether the connection line that Mark fed Kim was game or not, a true connection manifested over time. The friendship naturally progressed into a whirlwind romance. Before long, the two were married, and they were successful both at marriage and in their respective fields. Mark was an electrician and Kim was a well-respected psychologist. Life was just beginning. The couple had the world in the palm of their hands.

CHAPTER 2

"I should've seen this coming," Kim remarked. Mark chuckled as Kim held the home pregnancy test. The pink plus sign shone brightly. "Some doctor you are," Mark joked. "You don't even know when you're pregnant yourself."

"Hush, boy, you know I'm not that type of doctor." Kim looked at Mark with adoring eyes. "This completes our family, bae." Mark reached in and kissed her fully on the lips. After momentarily thinking about it, a revelation hit Mark. With furrowed eyebrows, he said, "You know what this means now, baby girl?"

Kim already suspected where this line of questioning was headed. Mark had been fussing about Kim kicking it with Stephanie as of late. Even if they didn't go out, Stephanie was still at their house. Now Mark had the perfect argument to support him: Kim's pregnancy. It wasn't that Mark didn't like Stephanie. He did. It was just that he was tired of her. He also occasionally fretted over the possibility of Stephanie's ways rubbing off on Kimberly.

"No, what does that mean, Mark?" Kim asked with much attitude. "This means that you won't be running your fast ass around all over the city," Mark answered with a look of triumph. "It also means that you got to get somewhere and sit your tail down. You are somebody's mama now. All that ripping and running with Stephanie is over. That's what that means," Mark said with a smile to soften the blow. "Look, Mark, I hear you and I respect you. But please understand that Steph is like a sister to me. I can't just shut her out. You're right about the running around part, but she's going to be in my life."

Mark didn't want to press the issue. He knew that the bond between the two women was solid. He chose to compromise. "Yeah, bae, I feel that, but she ain't got to be here 24/7. She needs to get herself a man. That's her problem. Stephanie needs to settle down with one man instead of ripping and running. That girl knows she needs to stop gallivanting all over the city. She wonders why men don't stay interested in her for so long. It ain't hard to tell, bae."

Kim was tired of hearing the same old song and dance. "Yeah, yeah, that's Steph's business. Enough of that. We need to be talking about this baby." Kim smiled. The nine months went by uneventfully. Mark and Kimberly Stevens were blessed with a beautiful baby girl. They christened her with the name of Essence Faith. Essence was a peaceful and happy baby. After a few weeks, Mark began to notice a change in Kim's attitude. He suspected that Kim was suffering from postpartum depression (PPD).

"Kim, sweetheart, what's going on with you?" Kim looked at Mark questioningly. "I'm saying, bae, it seems that you've been down lately." It was true; Kim was going through a little spell. She felt as though she was losing herself. Despite the majority's census, maternal instincts were not automatic for Kim. The dependence that Essence had on Kim was slightly overwhelming.

Kim felt as though she had let go of herself in order to give all of herself to Essence. She was going through a phase of shifting the balance of responsibility. Kim was also going through issues concerning her appearance. The baby had caused her to gain a considerable amount of weight as well as incurring stretch marks.

"I don't know what's going on with me, Mark. I just don't feel like myself lately."

Kim began to push Mark further and further away. Mark tried to be sympathetic, but over the course of time, the needs of his lower self plagued him. He was tormented with the desire for reciprocity. When Kim closed herself up in a shell, she closed off everything. She closed communication, nurturing, and her legs. The connection between her and Mark was out of synch.

"Don't touch me, Mark. No, get off of me." Once again, Kim shot down Mark's attempts at intimacy. "Don't be such a narcissistic ass, Mark. You only think of yourself." Again, Mark slunk away to the realm of the neglected.

****

"Damn," Paul said. "I'm surprised you kickin' it with a brotha." Paul was one of the few friends that Mark had. They'd been friends since their freshman year at Boys & Girls high school. "I'm saying, you must've snuck out. She can't know that you're hanging out with me. She thinks that your man is a straight up dog."

Since Mark and Kim's marriage years before, Mark didn't venture out with the boys too much. "Come on, P, it ain't like that, kid. You know that we still tight." Paul shook his head. "Whatever, man. All of a sudden you out kickin' it? Shit must be thick on the home front." With that being said, Mark put his head down in shame. Once again, Paul had been able to read the situation.

"I knew it, man. What in the world is going on with you and Kim?" Paul really couldn't understand the marriage life. After graduating college, Paul still chose to be single and childless. He reveled in his bachelorhood. "You don't understand, P."

This offended Paul. "What the fuck you mean I don't understand? What? Just because I'm not married, I can't understand? What's really going' on, bro?" asked P. After exhaling deeply, Mark decided to enlighten Paul about his household. "Listen, P, shit is crazy at the house right now. It's like Kim can't stand me. It's like a brother disgusts her." This puzzled Paul. "What you talking about, bro?"

"She can't stand for me to look at her, let alone touch her. She ain't let me touch her since the baby was born."

Paul calculated Essence's age. Four months. "What!" Paul exclaimed. "You mean to tell me you ain't had no power U, no punnani, no poo-tang, no pu-pu platter, no - "

"All right, all right, P, damn!"

Paul shook his head sadly. "Damn, Mark, I feel for you, man. Maybe you've got to give it time, bro. Maybe the baby caused a hormonal imbalance or something."

That night marked the beginning of hanging out for Mark and Paul. Mark felt neglected and unwanted at home. He found a respite of pleasure in hanging out with his homie Paul. He didn't quite understand what was going on with Kim, but he felt that her spell would pass soon.

Mark loved his wife and daughter. Kim and Essence were his universe. Mark only hung out with Paul to stamp out the void of loneliness. Kim's change also brought about a change in Mark. The frustration that he felt began to take its toll on him. He sought a release.

CHAPTER 3

"What the hell do you mean, James? You better tell me something, because I don't understand. I've been loyal to this company for years. Just like that you gonna up and let me go? The brother is always the first to go, right?"

Mark's supervisor James began to redden in the face. He had been chosen to tell Mark about him being laid off. Mark was usually mild-mannered and James felt as if he could handle Mark. Now that the news had been borne, James wasn't quite sure of himself any longer.

"All of these fuckin' years I put into this bullshit-ass company. Who worked overtime when no one else wanted to? Me, that's who! Who else got the bullshit vacation days no one else wanted? Me, that's who! Who always worked on the weekends? It was me! What about late night emergency calls? Once again it was fuckin' Mark."

James began to fidget and shuffle his feet. "Once again, Mark, I'm sorry. This was not my decision. Please keep in mind that this layoff is just temporary. Let me reiterate that I've just been chosen to be the bearer of bad news." James hoped that this would pacify Mark's rage.

"Yeah? Well fuck you, James! This ragtag penny ante-ass company can go down in flames for all I care. I can do better than this. You know it, and I know it."

Mark stormed out of the office with his pride still intact. The fact of the matter was that with the new addition to his family, Mark needed this job. With the country slowly crawling out of the recession, there weren't any good jobs available. Mark knew it was going to be a long road ahead of him.

****

Mark and Kim's life at home became more strained. Kim began to slip further into the pits of depression. The only positive thing about their whole ordeal was that her job performance wasn't suffering because of her issues. If anything, her performance thrived mainly because she immersed herself in her work. She did this in order to avoid her reality at home. Essence spent a lot of time with Kim's parents. They also noticed a change in Kim. This change propelled them to step in and care for Essence until Kim recovered from her issues.

"Damn, you scared me, Mark!" Kim was standing in the kitchen looking out into the backyard. As usual, she was in a catatonic-like state. "I didn't hear you creep up in here, boy." Mark had wrapped his arms around her waist. She knew that Mark didn't deserve the treatment, or lack thereof, but she couldn't control it. The feelings that she was experiencing totally consumed her.

Mark tried very hard to be sympathetic to what Kim was going through. "How are you feelin' today, bae?" Mark asked cautiously. He desired for the woman that he married to reappear. "I'm feeling fine, Mark. Baby, I know I haven't been myself lately. Sweetheart, don't think for one minute that I don't love you or Essence. I just don't know what the fuck is wrong with me. I feel like I'm losing my mind or something. I'm contemplating seeking some type of therapy." A colleague at work had already diagnosed Kim with acute postpartum depression. Kim was at the point of accepting this diagnosis. She suspected as much even though it didn't totally register with her.

"Baby, I know it's rough on you right now. Whatever we got to do, we'll do. What does your therapist friend say?" Mark asked. "She suggests that I go into treatment, beginning with a therapeutic community. The place is called Serenity. It's in the Catskill Mountains." Mark was taken aback. "What?" Mark couldn't fathom this. "You mean to tell me that she suggested that you leave Essence and me? I'll be damned! What kind of advice is that? How can you learn to deal with us by not dealing with us? Running away will not fix this shit, Kim."

"Mark, listen, baby. It's not you or Essence. I just have to get myself together. It's me. I need these three months so I can straighten this shit out in me. "Three months!" Mark exclaimed. "What about us? What am I supposed to do with Essence?" Mark was irate. "Calm down, Mark. My parents will help you with Essence. You can give them breaks from time to time. On visiting days, the both of you could come see me up at Serenity. We just can't go on the way we are. It is not your fault, Mark. I don't want you to think that any of this is your fault. I'm afraid though. I'm afraid if I don't do this I'll lose it all. I'll lose you, Essence, my career, and my mind."

Mark had no choice. He felt Kim's pain. He was so used to seeing Kim in charge and in control. He couldn't understand what was going on with her. He'd never seen a weakness expose itself in Kim, and seeing one now was mind-boggling. "Sweetheart, if that's what's absolutely needed, then so be it. We have to do what's best for us. I understand, bae."

They hugged, shed tears, and made each other promises. *Damn*, Mark thought. *First I lose my job, now it looks like I might lose my family. What the hell is going on? I don't understand life right now.*

****

"Mark, you, my man, are a beast. I can't believe that you are out here partying. You are going hard in the paint, bro." Paul was tickled at how Mark was handling his newfound freedom. He wasn't completely enlightened about Kim's whereabouts, but he knew she must have been missing in action. He also knew about Mark's unemployment situation and he suspected that Mark was going through a phase. "Come on, P, man, you know how we do. Brooklyn's in the house, without a doubt."

Paul chuckled. "Naw, I don't know how *we* do, I know how *I* do. Let me find out you tryna take my spot." They both laughed. Excuse me, fellas." Both Paul and Mark looked up to see a fine specimen of sheer beauty. Since Paul was a bachelor, he felt he was bound by duty to take the lead.

"My name is Paul, and this is my partner Mark." Paul extended his hand. "What can I do for you, beautiful?" The whole while the picture of perfection kept her eyes trained on Mark. "My name is Alexis, and I was wondering if a sister could join you."

Mark spotted the interest in Alexis's eyes. During normal times in his life he wouldn't have entertained the current situation. However, these were no longer normal times in his life. "Pleasure to meet you, Alexis," Mark replied. "It would also be a pleasure to be graced with your hypnotic beauty."

Paul looked at Mark with both shock and awe. He was surprised at Mark's newfound transformation. Alexis positioned herself between Mark and Paul. She turned to face Mark directly. "So can a girl buy you a drink?" Mark didn't have any intention of pursuing any romantic relationships, but he felt that a platonic one couldn't hurt. With Kim in treatment at Serenity and with the months of neglect on her part, Mark was starved for female energy. "I'd appreciate that, Alexis. I'm drinking Hennessy neat."

Paul, feeling a little dejected, butted in, "I'm drinking gin and juice. "Alexis gave him a polite but firm look to let him know that he wasn't her type of hype. "Okay, gentlemen, Hennessy neat and gin and juice coming up." The waiters tripped over themselves to attend to the beautiful Alexis. "So Mark…" Alexis turned her attention back to Mark. "What's your story?" Mark couldn't hide the fact that he was married. His diamond wedding ring was evidence of the fact. Since he was only looking for a friend, he was open.

"Well, Alexis, my story is a long one. How much time do you have?" he asked jokingly.

"I have as much time as you need," she answered seductively.

At that, Mark had to suppress his K-9 hormones. "As you can see, Alexis," Mark began, motioning to his ring, "I'm married." Alexis acknowledged this. "Yes, I noticed that, Mark. I was wondering what woman in her right mind would let such a fine man out to a club by himself." *If only you knew*, thought Mark.

Alexis and Mark talked and laughed until the wee hours of the morning. Paul had long since gone home. Alexis and Mark had been prompted to leave the club. After that they ventured to Carmichael's diner on Guy R. Brewer. "Mark, I must say, you are like a breath of fresh air."

Mark was feeling the same about her as well. She was what you would consider petite. She put you in the mind frame of Jada Pinkett-Smith. Alexis's dark skin was smooth and as soft as a baby's bottom. Her naturally curly hair with its blond highlights was close-cropped. Her beauty was effulgent, but her dark eyes told a story of its own.

****

Alexis's dark eyes told a story that was equivalent to that of her dark, turbulent past. Alexis was raised in a two parent household, but it wasn't a household of love. Instead, it was a house of horror with the main attraction being that of sexual abuse. Evelyn, Alexis's mother, remarried a man named Sam when Alexis was nine years old. Sam moved them from the ghetto in Brooklyn to the posh Jamaica Estates in Queens. Once Sam trapped them in his domain, the sexual deviance began. He started with a seemingly innocent pat on her bottom at the age of nine to all out sexual abuse until the age of sixteen. At sixteen, Alexis couldn't take it anymore. Sam tried to force himself on her sweet sixteenth day. Alexis finally fought back and as a result, she killed him.

Evelyn overlooked the fact that her innocent child, since the age of nine, began to change. She was blinded by the fact that she was no longer living in squalor. Sam owned two successful clothing stores in the city. He kept Evelyn living far above her usual means. With her head up in the clouds, she was oblivious to her daughter's reality. The day Alexis fought back was the day Evelyn was brought back down to earth. In the blink of an eye, her maternal duty of protection was reinstalled.

When the cops arrived at Jamaica Estates, Evelyn took full responsibility for the murder. She stated that she had caught her husband in the act of molesting her daughter. She claimed that she had snapped and grabbed a ball peen hammer. Evelyn claimed that she had blacked out and couldn't remember a thing. She claimed to be caught up in a crime of passion. Fortunately for Alexis, the story was believable. Alexis was taken to the doctor and he corroborated the fact that Alexis was traumatized due to sexual assault.

In Sam's twisted mind, he loved Alexis. Through the fog of depression, he knew that he was assassinating her spirits. In a brief flash of clarity, while he was crafting his will, he named Alexis as his beneficiary. He hoped that this would right some of the wrongs he had bestowed upon her. Along with monetary compensation, Alexis was also given two of the three stores that Sam owned. This would indeed cover her financially, but in no way could it cover her emotional scars.

****

"I must say, Mark that it was a pleasure meeting you. As I stated earlier, you, boyfriend, are a breath of fresh air. If it's cool, I'd like to continue our newfound friendship." Alexis had a devilish, yet seductive look about her.

"Friend, huh?" Mark chuckled. "I'll ask my wife and see if it's cool if I have a beautiful girlfriend," Mark joked. At this, they both laughed. "Seriously though, Alexis, it's cool. At this point in my life, that's probably what I need." Alexis looked hopeful. "So you need a new friend, huh?"

"Yeah, no doubt, especially a female. You may be able to give me some insight into what's going wrong in my marriage." "What are friends for?" Alexis said. In her head, she thought, *Friendship is the first step to a relationship. So friends we are.*

CHAPTER 4

"So baby girl, how are you holding up?" It was finally visiting day for Kim. "I'm good, bae. Lord knows that I miss you and Essence. I feel so guilty that I'm here. I feel like I've abandoned y'all. Just let me get myself together, bae. As soon as possible, I'll be back and better than ever."

Mark looked at his wife through pain-ridden eyes. "Just chill, baby. Don't stress about us. We're doing all right. Right now we just need to get you back to you. Essence and I are okay, but like you said, do what you have to do so it'll be better when this is over." "Mark, what the therapist came up with so far makes a little sense."

Mark loved his wife with everything in him. He was definitely interested in Kim's progress. "What's up, Kim? What did ole boy say?" "He said that me being sheltered my whole life was the key factor that led to my condition." Mark looked doubtful. "How did he come up with that?" he asked. "Well, he said that I wasn't prepared for any adversity. He says that I've been blinded and desensitized to real-life issues."

Mark thought on what he knew Kim's past to be. Her parents, Mr. and Mrs. Upright, were just as their name suggested: upright and upstanding. Kim adored her parents, especially her father. She looked up to him so much that she chose the same path as him. Like Kim, Mr. Upright was also a doctor. He was a psychologist and Mrs. Upright was an educator. Financially, they were a well-off family. Kim's parents devoted themselves to her. They blocked the savage world and replaced it with their very own brand of fairytale. Everything seemed perfect in the Upright household. Dr. Upright made all of the major decisions in the home. He fit the mold of an old-school husband and father. He shielded his woman from any drama, stress, or adversity the world might bring. "Yeah," Kim replied. "The doctor said since I was obsessively sheltered, the minute I was confronted with new issues or adversity, I shut down. He said it was because I was stripped of the reasoning to deal with things. Therefore, I defended myself by retreating. Think about it, Mark. I've never had to deal with too much. I've never been forced to make decisions. Even now, you make most of the decisions." Mark had to agree with this.

"So I never had to be responsible for myself, let alone a baby. Then on top of that, when I look in the mirror, I feel so disgusting." At that, Mark objected. "That's not true, bae, you still all that. Shit, if anything, the pregnancy made you even finer." He meant every word he said.

"Come on, Mark, you don't have to patronize me. I am not blind. I've gotten mad, fat, and I have these hideous-looking stretch marks. I realize that I've sunken into a deep depression, and I realize that I must pull myself out." "All right, baby, I understand. Just know you don't have to pull yourself out alone. I'm here for you, boo."

"I know, bae-bae. I'm grateful for that too. Trust me though, I have to do it on my own. I can no longer allow myself to be sheltered. I must come out of the shell and deal with life head-on. If I don't learn to address things on my own, then anytime something arises this 'spell' can happen again. Just be patient, baby. I'll be home before you know it, and when it happens, it'll be better off for all of us. I'll be a stronger woman. Until then, continue to hold me down, and help Momma and Daddy take care of Essence Faith."

****

Mark left Serenity feeling depressed himself. He hated to see the love of his life in this state. He never viewed Kim as weak, but he understood the doctor's theory. He could see how Kim's upbringing and sheltering could produce the current effect on her. Mark drove straight home. It was pouring down raining and this added to his melancholy mood. After drinking a couple glasses of cognac, he dozed off in his favorite recliner. Mark was awakened by the doorbell chimes. He was disoriented at first. The living room was in complete darkness. "Damn,

I must've slept at least three hours." The doorbell chimed again. Mark was dumbfounded because he wasn't expecting anybody. Add that to the fact that it was late and it stupefied him. "Who is it?" Mark yelled as he approached the door. He pulled open the door without receiving an answer.

Standing at the front door in the pouring down rain was Stephanie. "Steph? What are you doin' out here in all this rain?" Mark stood back to let Stephanie enter the house. He noticed that she wobbled a bit as she walked. "Just out and about," she slurred. "I decided I'd come check up on shit." Mark chuckled. "What? You makin' sure I ain't creeping on ya girl?" "Damn right!" Stephanie said. It was evident that Stephanie was drunk. "Steph, why are you out driving like that?"

Stephanie was beyond inebriated. She had gone to the bar on her quest and she was a few drinks past her limit. She plopped down on the couch. "Yeah, yeah, save it, Mark, I'm a big girl." Mark walked to the linen closet to retrieve a blanket for Stephanie. When he came back to the living room, she was snoring slightly. "Look at this lush." Mark quietly covered her up with a blanket.

Mark retreated to his bedroom. He was drained both physically and mentally. Not only was Kim's situation taxing on him, but his job situation was also. He and Kim had savings stacked up, but with no income coming in, it was dwindling down fast. Those pressing issues were on Mark's mind before he dozed off for the second time that night. Deep into Mark's slumber, he began to dream. "Uh, that feels so good, baby. I'm so glad you're finally home. I missed you so much, baby. Damn, I can tell you must've missed daddy too."

Kim was giving Mark the best blow job that she had ever given him. She licked him from his base all the way up to the tip of his shaft. Kim's mouth was working like a vacuum pump. As she deep throated him, she hummed on his member, causing a tingling vibration. "Don't stop, baby girl!" Mark cried out in his sleep "I won't stop, baby."

This gave Mark pause, because Kim didn't sound like herself. In the throes of ecstasy, Mark felt himself about to explode. At that very moment, she stopped. Mark felt a weight come upon him as she mounted him. This shift caused Mark to fully awaken.

"What the fuck?" Mark pushed the body off him and jumped up to find Stephanie butt naked in his bed. "Stephanie, what the fuck are you doin'?" Stephanie looked at Mark, nonplussed. "What? Mark, don't front, you was enjoying yourself. Now all of a sudden in the middle of it you catch a conscience?"

It was Mark's turn to look perplexed. "What the hell are you talking about? I thought I was dreaming this shit." Stephanie laughed coldly. "Naw, sweetheart, I just made your dreams come true." Mark couldn't believe Stephanie. He'd been sexually deprived as of late, but he couldn't disrespect Kim by sleeping with her girl. "You really trippin', Steph," Mark said while gathering his clothes. "Get dressed and meet me in the living room. We got to clear this up."

Stephanie couldn't believe that Mark was turning her down. She reluctantly went into the living room. Before Mark could go face her in the living room, he had to throw cold water on his face. He couldn't believe Stephanie. *Damn*, he thought, *Stephanie is off the fucking chain. She got a mean head game though.* He chuckled.

When he stepped into the living room, he was broadsided, finding Stephanie spread-eagled on the floor and pleasuring herself. She moaned out loud as she played with her magic button. Her face revealed pure bliss as she continued to seduce Mark. "Come get some of these sugar walls, Mark." Stephanie wasn't used to being turned down by men. Mark had been the first, and now she was determined to make him submit to her advances.

Mark couldn't believe his eyes when Stephanie began to squirt. "Uh-uh, Steph, get your ass up. We ain't going there." Stephanie ignored him as she continued to pleasure herself. She noticed the tent that Mark made in his sweatpants. "Your mouth may be telling me to stop, but your magic stick says the opposite, Mark."

Mark was embarrassed that Stephanie had busted him out like that. "Look, Steph, that shit you doin' is mad foul. How you gonna disrespect Kim like that in her own house? Y'all supposed to be like sisters and shit. You one trifling bitch. Now get ya nasty ass up and get out of my house."

This snapped Stephanie back to reality. "Wait, Mark, hold on. Let me speak my peace." Stephanie jumped up off of the floor and quickly got dressed. She looked at Mark with eyes that were filled with sorrow. "Like I said, Mark, let me help you understand, then I'm out of the door." Mark looked at her with skepticism. "I promise, Mark, just let me explain."

Stephanie definitely had an effect on Mark. If it would have been anyone else besides Stephanie, he would've gone there. This episode just showed Mark how vulnerable he was. "Before you think sideways about me, let me say that I don't know what got into me. Yeah, I got toasted on the drink earlier, but I'm not gonna use that as an excuse. We're both grown, and I'm not gonna play any games with you, Mark." Stephanie took a deep breath and then exhaled.

"The truth of the matter is that I felt you from day one. Remember when we met in the club? I tried to get with you then. I saw it your eyes, Mark. You were feeling me too. Then bam, you passed over me for Kim. When I see the life that Kim and you have, I can't help but feel like Kim stole my life. It's supposed to be you and me married with a child. All of this time I've been holding this in. This has been my cross to bear. I love Kim like a sister, but when I see what y'all have, I get a tad bit envious. I guess I just wanted to sample the goods. Just wanted to see what I was missing. A part of me wanted to show you what you were missing as well." After Stephanie spoke her piece, she was drained. The reality of her actions was now present on her face. The sorrow was replaced with fear. "Hopefully we can keep this episode between us, Mark. You may not believe me after that stunt I pulled, but I do love Kim. For a brief moment I allowed my selfishness to lead me to perform this indiscretion. Hopefully we can get past this. Trust me. It will never happen again."

Stephanie's raw honesty and truth melted away Mark's anger. She jumped up with tears in her eyes as she rushed past Mark. As she reached the front door, she looked back at Mark once more. The look of dejection was ever present on her face.

Mark was never one to crush the fragile female's esteem or ego. "Don't sweat it, Steph. This shit stays between us. Who knows?" Mark smiled. "Maybe next lifetime." This brought a smile to Stephanie's face as she continued out the door. Mark tossed and turned for the remainder of the night. His sleeplessness drove him to call Alexis.

CHAPTER 5

Kim's progress was coming along nicely. Serenity was one of the top therapeutic facilities in the entire northeast. Kim was most definitely benefitting from their program.

Mark, on the other hand, was quickly regressing. The absence of his wife pushed him into a relationship, albeit a platonic one, with Alexis. Like a lot of things in life it began innocently on his part, but then it evolved into what should've never been. Unbeknownst to Mark, Alexis plotted each move like a master chessman. She used Mark's current situation and lack of spousal attention to her advantage.

"I'm saying, Alexis. Something's got to give. I can't find a job and I'm damn near flat broke. I got bills, a mortgage, a new baby, and to top it all off, my wife is in a crazy house. I swear, Lex, I'm 'bout ready to take it to the streets."

Before Mark married Kimberly and studied to be an electrician, he and Paul were both full-fledged in the streets. They were hardened as they were embroiled on the mean streets of Brooklyn. This was a world that they were currently removed from, but desperate times called for desperate measures. He now considered pursuing the street life as a means to an end. This was nothing new to Mark. It was like riding a bike. In that world the players changed, but the game remained the same.

Alexis attempted to lighten the mood jokingly. "What you know about them streets, boy?" Mark looked at her like she was crazy. "Come on, ma, how many guys you know from Do or Die Bed-Stuy that ain't been in them streets at some point in their life? See, you a Queens girl. It may be a little different for y'all, but for us Brooklynites, that's life."

Mark's statements ruffled Alexis's feathers. "For your information, Mr. Gangster, I'm from 'never ran, never will', the Hill in Brownsville. So you should know that I saw it all. As a matter of fact, since you from the Stuy, you should know my cousin Rondue from Saratoga Avenue."

The name Rondue sparked recognition in Mark's eyes. "Yeah, I remember Rondue. We used to go to Boys & Girls high school together. I remember him getting kicked out though. I heard he was gettin' it now." Alexis nodded her head. "Yeah, he gettin' it. That's my first cousin. We're two sisters' kids."

Mark shook his head. "Is that right?" "Yeah, that's right. We tight like siblings though. That boy will do anything for me." Alexis knew that she had already sown the seed She knew that if hard times continued to befall Mark then he would broach the subject of a hookup. Alexis felt like if she plugged him in, then he would be indebted to her. In her eyes, this would prove that she was loyal and down for him. Alexis wanted to show him that she could be his ride-or-die chick. She felt as though that act would solidify her position in Mark's world. She wanted to play Bonnie to Mark's Clyde.

She didn't know what it was that attracted her so much to Mark. Because of her past experience with her stepfather, she was usually reserved around men. Maybe it was just the right time, maybe her biological clock was ticking, or maybe Mark was the one. Whatever the case, Alexis was compelled to give it a try. She never opened up to any man, but she felt safe with Mark. Mark was chosen, but he wasn't even aware of it. They hadn't crossed over the platonic line as of yet, but that was definitely in her plans.

"Okay, okay, Ms. Thang, so what, now you're a gangstress?" Alexis decided to be sarcastic, yet truthful. "Come on, son, I'm from Brooklyn. How many people you know from Brooklyn who ain't got a li'l gangster in 'em?"

This reality caused Mark to chuckle. "You a wild girl, Lexis. You're mad cool. Let me get on the personal tip though if you don't mind." Alexis just nodded her head in approval. "Alexis, you're a bad chick, without a doubt. You got your own business, you a dime piece with a phat body, got a good head on your shoulders… What I wanna know is, what are you doing still single?"

Alexis was used to this line of questioning. She even expected it. Her mother Evelyn even asked this question at least once a week. She was ready for some grandchildren and for Alexis to settle down, but she knew that because of her deceased husband Sam, Alexis had her share of issues with men. "Well, Mark, to tell you the truth, up until now I haven't found a man that was worthy. That's why I'm single." Mark furrowed his brows, almost oblivious to the innuendo. "Up until now? You shouldn't be alone, ma. I know that you don't need a man, but you should at least experience love once."

Again she looked at Mark intently. "That, boyfriend, is indeed a sister's goal, trust and believe."

****

Mark and Alexis continued to grow closer to each other. In Kim's absence, he was starved and longing for female energy. Alexis was the outlet that Mark seriously needed. "Listen, Mark, we need to talk." Mark sensed the seriousness in Alexis's tone. He exhaled the marijuana smoke and paid rapt attention. She proceeded to openly confide in him. She opened up her total self to Mark and explained why she didn't trust men because of her stepfather.

Alexis, after divulging her innermost secrets to Mark, blew him away. He felt privileged that she would discuss her private life with him. From the outside looking in, he would have never guessed in a million years that she was so fragile. Her fragility and vulnerability served to intensify the magnetic energy Mark felt from her. Mark leaned in and gently kissed Alexis, and for the first time, they crossed the platonic line. At first, Alexis was caught off guard but after a moment, she reciprocated. The kiss was light, sweet, and quick. "Where did that come from?"

Mark was asking himself the same question. When he felt the magnetic force pull him close to Alexis, he didn't have the resistance to pull back. He gave into his feelings because he was too weak to fight them. "I-I…" Mark stammered. "I'm sorry, Alexis. I don't know what got into me." Mark's shyness tickled Alexis. "There's no need to apologize to me, Mark. I'm grown, and in case you didn't notice, I responded to your advances." This brief encounter sparked off a romantic whirlwind between the two. From that day forward, they were inseparable.

****

"Good news, baby!" Kim was not only smiling, but she was looking good, and she was in a great mood as well. As soon as Mark entered the visiting area, she jumped into his arms. "Baby, I've completed the necessary steps in order to be released." This was pleasing to Mark's ears. He missed his wife immensely. In the back of his mind, he heard a nudging voice that tormented him about Alexis. He figured he'd cross that bridge when he got there. "Really, baby? That's what's up! I'm so glad to hear that, sweetheart. Your man missed you so much. I'm glad you're back to your old self. Essence misses you too, baby. She looks just like you too. Kim, baby, I can't wait to get you home."

Kim had that knowing look on her face. "I can't wait to get home either. Let's go get my stuff and sign this paperwork so we can bounce. Mark, I feel so invigorated, so free. I have a new lease on life. It's time for me to shed the old me. It is time for me to step out of my comfort zone and not be so sheltered. It's time for me to live, baby."

****

While Kim was getting settled in again at home and work, Mark was busy juggling his household as well as Alexis. He informed Alexis of Kim's return. The reality of Kim's re-emergence refueled Alexis's drive in obtaining Mark's heart. Alexis catered to Mark every day in every way. She fed his ego, his sexual desires, and she motivated him with encouragement.

Kim, on the flip side of the coin, was the total opposite. She constantly complained that Mark needed to gain employment. Kim was unsympathetic to his plight. Since returning home from Serenity she was outspoken, domineering, and a diva. Mark was quickly growing tired of her.

****

"I'm saying, Alexis, I'm tired of this shit. The whole world is on my back: the bill collectors, the bank, and to top it off, Kim too. She acts like I'm some deadbeat that enjoys not working. It's bad enough being married to a big-time doctor, but it's even worse when you're unemployed." Alexis nodded her head in understanding. "I feel you, Mark. So what you come up with? If you want, you can manage one of the shops."

Mark cringed at the suggestion. "I appreciate the offer, Lex, but I can't have you taking care of me." Once again, Alexis nodded her head knowingly. "I respect that, Mark. So what you gonna do?" Mark sighed. "Remember a while ago when I told you that I was gonna have to take it back to the streets?" Alexis nodded her response. "Well, that's what I gotta do to elevate up outta this situation."

Alexis had already figured that Mark would go that route. She expected that he wouldn't accept the job offer from her. Mark was a proud man, unlike a lot of men who would've jumped at the handout. "Well, baby, you know I'm down for you."

That statement resonated within Mark. "Yeah, I feel that, Alexis. That's why I'm into you so much. Listen, I do need a favor though." Alexis already knew what was coming. "I need you to plug me into Rondue." "That's a done deal, baby. I got you."

****

Mark and Alexis walked into the world-famous Junior's restaurant on Flatbush Avenue. It took Rondue a few days to get back to Alexis because he was out of town. After she fussed at him about taking so long to call back, she set up the meeting. Rondue spotted his cousin Alexis coming into Junior's. She turned heads and demanded attention wherever she went. He also spotted Mark. Mark looked familiar to him, but he couldn't place him.

"Hey Ronnie, what's good?" Alexis was the only one Rondue allowed to call him Ronnie. "Hey, sexy Lexy. What up, duke?" he said, acknowledging Mark. "What's up, Rondue? It's been a long time." Rondue was taken aback. He bristled at Mark's statement because it caught him off guard. He thought to himself, *What the hell Alexis got me crossed up in?* He glared at Alexis for some reassurance. He didn't know if Mark was some joker from back in the day who sought revenge or what. "What you mean it's been a long time, Duke? Where you know me from, playboy?"

Mark sensed the change in Rondue's demeanor. "Chill, man, it's me, Mark. We used to go to the Boys & Girls together." Rondue looked closer at Mark. "Shit, Marky Mark? Damn, son, you put on some weight. I'm used to you being a little skinny, pimple-faced youth. You done got all diesel and shit. What, you just getting off lock?"

Mark was relieved that Rondue remembered him. "Naw, man. Shit, I wouldn't wish that on my worst enemy." Rondue turned to Alexis. "Lexy, you shoulda seen this kid - him and his partner Paul. They thought they were Run-DMC and shit." At this, the trio laughed. The laughter was necessary in order to dispel the cloud of tension. "You right, Mark, it's been a long time." Rondue looked at his watch. "Reunions are good, but time is loot."

This prompted Alexis to begin her spiel. "I know that Ronnie, and that's why I'm grateful for you meeting us." Rondue knew his cousin like a book. The second she called him Ronnie, he knew that there was some shit in the game. "Cut the bullshit, Alexis, what's the deal? I know you ain't got me out here for some class reunion shit."

"Damn, Ronnie, it's like that? Listen, Mark is my man, and - " At this revelation, Rondue was taken aback. Alexis claiming a man and letting him meet him was a newsworthy event. "Hold up, Lexy, ya man? As in man, man?" Rondue joked, wiggling his eyebrows.

"Hush up, boy! That's right, my man. The thing is, he fell on hard times at work. He wants to get in the game, so I figured you could help him." Rondue looked at Alexis like she was crazy. "Please, Ronnie, this is the first and last time I come at you like this." Mark hated to hear Alexis pleading to Rondue on his behalf. He decided to speak up. "Yeah, Rondue, what Alexis is saying is true. Shit is thick for me right now. I still got a little change left, but if I don't invest it, I'm gonna be assed out. So what up, Rondue? You got a spot for me or what?"

Rondue took a second to size Mark up. "A'ight, rule number one, don't have your woman all up in your business. When it comes to these streets, keep her out of it." Rondue looked at Alexis. "Lexy, go over there and order yourself a cheesecake. Give us time to talk."

****

After the initial meeting, everything fell into place. Mark was a natural-born hustler. After getting acclimated to life, he found his niche. Rondue let him invest his money and helped him set up shop in Tompkins projects. Rondue even loaned him three of his soldiers 'til he got on his feet. In return for this, Mark was obligated to score only from Rondue.

On the strength of Alexis, Rondue firmly supported and backed Mark. Rondue took the time to cultivate Mark into a certified player in the game. Alexis, on the other hand, felt like she had cemented herself into Mark's heart. She proved that she could be the woman that he needed, the ride-or-die chick that you always hear about. Alexis was leaving her mark and staking her claim.

Kimberly noticed a change in Mark. Not only was he keeping strangers and later hours, but he also possessed large sums of unaccounted-for money. His attitude had even changed. He had grown colder as he morphed into the person that the streets breed. He had not yet learned how to turn the persona on and off. She didn't know what Mark was going through, but she knew she didn't like it. Their home life once again was strained. Her newfound peace was fragile and her upbringing hadn't prepared her for Mark's new chosen life.

Alexis, however, ingrained herself into Mark's new life. She reveled in her position as Bonnie to Mark's Clyde. Rondue took notice of Alexis's constant presence. There were days when he would drop by 77 Tompkins Avenue and Alexis would be coming through. Her refined beauty was out of place amongst the typical Reebok chicks. One day she was picking up money. Another time she was bringing Mark some food. At first, Rondue overlooked it, but because of its continuity, he spoke on it.

"Listen, Mark, with all due respect, homie, Alexis can't be coming through like this. Remember I told you about rule number one? We out here amongst some snakes and ruthless muh'fuckas. They'll use Alexis to get the drop on you." Mark was listening to everything that Rondue was saying.

"I'm saying, Mark, I know you know how to handle your B-I. The thing is, these streets are a different beast. What if the po-po's bag her? You think she could stand up under the pressure? The less she knows the better. Besides, she's like my little sister. I don't want her involved in our bullshit. You gots to fix this shit, Mark." "You right, Rondue. That's good shit you spittin'. I'm on it."

CHAPTER 6

When Mark entered the house, he was taken aback. Kim had the lights dimmed low, the Isley Brothers crooning "Between the Sheets", and she appeared to be clothed in the master art of seduction. The living room exhibited the precise definition of romantic ambiance.

"Well, well, well. What have we here?" Mark was digging what he was seeing. "What brought on all of this?" Mark asked, waving hands. "I just wanted to cater to my man, that's all." Kim knew that hers and Mark's relationship was lacking lately. She swore she felt the passion draining with each passing day. With everything in her, she was determined to restore the fire. "Come on in here, boy, and let me take care of you." She led Mark into the master bathroom. Once inside, she began to undress him with the care which only love could provide. She drew him a hot bath and activated the jets in the tub.

While Kim was preparing to pamper Mark, he was in turmoil. His conscience plagued him due to his secretive new lifestyle. "Mark, I know things are strained between us right now. We hardly communicate anymore and we barely make love nowadays. It feels like we're just two ships passing in the night. When you're coming, I'm going, and vice versa. I know that I've been nagging you a lot lately. I know that I've been on your back, baby. I'm aware that I've been acting like this bitch from hell too. I realize that by me acting as such, it only drives us further apart.

When I went through my episode, you were right by my side. Now you're going through your thing and how do I repay you? I bitch, I piss, and I moan. Sweetheart, if you can find it in your beautiful heart to forgive me, we can move forward and fix our marriage. We can right the wrongs, and fix the damage."

Kim's words wreaked havoc on Mark's already-plagued conscience. Little did Kim know that Mark had been partaking in that which was forbidden. He'd forgone his vows and now embarked on a path that was once taboo to him.

Kim retrieved him from his internal strife by placing wet kisses on his neck. "You're right, Kim. We have been trippin' with each other lately. The way to be the best parents to Essence is by being the best we can be to each other. By the way, where is Essence anyway?"

Kim giggled. "She's with my parents, baby. We need this time alone. There are a lot of things that have been neglected." She batted her eyes at him in a coquettish manner. "We need some us time." With that, Mark pulled her into the tub with him. "Watch my hair!"

Her protests were quickly extinguished by Mark's passionate kisses. Her pleas turned into soft moans. Once the fire was ignited, the soft moans made way for heavy breathing. "Damn, baby, you got me open like we are teenagers and shit." Mark pulled the straps to Kim's salacious top-down and lightly made circles with his tongue around her areolas. He flicked the tip of his tongue over her elongated nipples. Kim vibrated with delight. With a sharp intake of breath, Kim said, "Boy, you know that's my spot. What are you tryna do to me?"

Mark only grunted his acknowledgment as he stayed on task. He continued to bathe her neck and breasts with wet kisses. In between kisses, Kim managed to find her voice. "Baby, I wanted tonight to be all about you." Kim's voice was husky and it served to drive Mark's desire. "No, Kim, it's all about us tonight. Stand up for me, sweets."

Kim did what was asked of her. Her negligee was dripping wet. Mark peeled it off like one would peel a banana. With Kim standing over him and soap suds running down her Coke bottle frame, Mark resumed his oral massage. He began with her pedicured toes and slowly worked his way upward. Kim had to brace herself on the towel rack to hold herself steady. When

Mark made his way to her thighs, her legs buckled with anticipation of what was to come. A chorus of soft ooh's escaped Kim's lips.

Her breathing was accelerated and her heart was beating as hard as an African drum. Its rhythm was conducted by the mouth of her husband. The conductor had worked her into a frenzy-like state. Mark gripped Kim's ample derriere and teased her bottom with his searing hot tongue.

"Damn you, Mark, stop teasing!" she hissed.

Mark knew his wife. He knew that she was fixated on receiving oral sex. It was her most naughty pleasure. "Eat up all of Mama's sugar, baby." Mark obliged his wife's request. Kim usually climaxed quickly when she received cunnilingus and tonight there wasn't any deviation from the norm.

Mark carried her into the bedroom. Upon entering the bedroom, Mark was once again taken aback. The aromatherapy candles were on blast and placed all around the bed. The sheer curtains on their canopy bed were at full mast. The breeze from the open windows caused the curtains to do a seductive dance. Upon the king-sized bed were several multicolored rose petals. Through the speakers Marvin was heard talking about sexual healing.

"You hear Marvin Gaye, baby? That's what we need right now, some sexual healing. I'm hot just like an oven and I need some loving." They were both basking in the afterglow of their lovemaking. Mark put the pound game on him like his life depended on it. In a sense, his life did depend on it. His married life was hanging on by a thin string. Before drifting off into a blissful sleep, his conscience took another jab at him. He knew he possessed what most men would kill for. He had a wife that was beautiful, fine, and on top of that, she was a doctor. She was caked up. After seeing Kim's rededication to their marriage, he decided to clean up his mess.

****

The next few days the twosome acted like newlyweds all over again. They were both recommitted to their marriage. During this time Mark was distant from Alexis. One night after a passionate lovemaking episode, Mark's phone rang. "Mark, who in the hell is calling you this late?" Mark knew that it could be one of three people. It was either Rondue, Yosef (one of Rondue's soldiers who was on loan to Mark), or Alexis. "Hold on, love, let me go answer the horn." This infuriated Kim. "What, you think I'm a fool or something, Mark? Why are you getting late-night calls? Furthermore, why do you have to leave my presence to go answer it?

You trying to play me, nigga?" Kim was trying to repair their marriage, but she had suspicions. For the sake of peace, she suppressed them, but due to the current situation, they were raging once again. There was still an issue of the unaccounted-for money and Mark's late night excursions. Now, to top it all off, he was getting late-night phone calls that he had to excuse himself for. "Just chill, Kim, and let me take this call. After I'm done, there are some things I need to discuss with you."

Kim continued to mutter her disagreements as Mark retrieved his phone. He screened the caller ID as Yosef's number appeared. "Yo, what up, homie?" Mark answered. "Ain't nothing, duke, everything peace on my end. But peep this though: you got company over here." This stumped Mark. "What you talking about 'Sef ?" Yosef chuckled. "Man, you greener than a pool table and twice as square. Listen, Duke, Alexis over here tripping." Yosef passed Alexis the phone.

"I don't know what kind of game you're playing, Mark, but you got me twisted. I know that you screening your calls and ain't answering mine. You must think I'm some bum bitch or something." Mark hated to be caught off guard. Alexis was right. When her number appeared on

Mark's caller ID, he'd let it go to his voicemail. "Chill out, Lex. Stop all that. I'll meet you around 12 tomorrow at the shop. You tripping and shit calling me all late. What up with that, yo? Let me find out you can't play your position." This statement sobered Alexis up. "I can play mine; just make sure you can play yours.

I ain't tryna blow up the spot, but you really playing games. In case you didn't know, I ain't the one to be playin' with. Twelve o'clock tomorrow, Mark, I'm not playing." Alexis hung up. When he returned to the bedroom, all the lights were on. Kim was sitting up in the bed with her arms folded. Her face was all scrunched up and her lips were turned up. "You ain't gotta look like that, sweets. I know you want answers…"

She interrupted him. "Naw, I don't want answers. I want the truth." "All right, I understand that, I feel that. Know this though, Kim: the truth isn't made to please." Kim interrupted again. "I'm not trying to be pleased. I'm trying to understand what the hell is going on." Mark took a deep breath and then exhaled. "I understand your position, ma. Now sit back and listen. Unscrew your face and put a pause on your attitude." This only caused Kim to scrunch up her face more and suck her teeth. As she rolled her neck, she said, "Save all that preamble and come on with the real."

Mark just shook his head as he gathered his thoughts. He knew that Kim was fed up and her attitude showed it. She gave him the evil eye as she waited for an explanation. "Listen, Kim, I'm gonna get to the point, but first, just hear me out. You know that you and I came from two different worlds. It's like our two worlds collided and now we walk down this same path together." Once again Kim sucked her teeth. "Kill the philosophy act, Mark. What are you saying? "Just chill, Kim, and follow me. Like I was saying, it's like our backgrounds are night and day. You had two parents who were prominent."

This was a worn-out assessment in Kim's eyes. She was sick and tired of people using her upbringing against her. "Here we go with this shit again."

"Naw, Kim, that's real shit. Anyway, just listen. You know they say opposites attract, right? Well, you had parents, upper middle class, they got money, careers, and shit. I don't. You went to college, medical school. You followed your old man's footsteps. You've been sheltered from my world, Kim. I, on the other hand, had one mother who was a heroin addict. Her career was that of prostitution. While y'all was upper middle class, we were the lowest of the low class. Y'all had a big house; we had a cramped apartment in Marcy Projects. Y'all had money to blow, while I was only able to steal a couple of food stamps before Moms shot it up. So yeah, we traveled different roads."

Kim was listening intently. She saw the passion in Mark through the picture he painted with his words. She knew that she was blessed because of her upbringing. At the same time, that blessing served as a curse as well. Because of that sheltering, she was unable to deal with life's curve balls.

"So yeah, Kim, shit was rough for me. We couldn't even keep a TV. Every time the monkey on her back whispered, she'd sell the TV for some smack. So early on I chose a means that I felt was justified. I chose street life, Kim. Me and Paul at a young age started scrambling. It either was that or starve. The thing is, I didn't stop until I finished electrical school."

Kim thought to herself, *That's exactly when we met.*

"So I said that to say this: when shit gets thick in life, we go into what the laws of nature call survival mode. Well, Kim, in case you haven't noticed yet, shit is now thick. I've been out of work forever and a day. We got bills and we have a new baby. You are on my back constantly. I was beginning to feel like I was less than a man. I had no income coming in and you were at

Serenity. So what do I do, baby? I go into survival mode." Kim was beginning to see the story unfold. "No, baby!" "Yes, Kim, I went back to what I know. I took it back to the streets."

Kim shook her head sadly as she tried her damnedest to blink back the tears. Mark held her in his arms and tried to console her. After what seemed like an eternity, Kim finally spoke. "So that explains it. That explains the late-night excursions, the unaccounted-for money, and the late-night calls. Boy, have you lost your damn mind?"

They continued to talk long into the night. Mark felt a little relieved now that Kim knew this secret. However, he still had one more secret: Alexis.

****

Mark stepped into the boutique to find Alexis hanging up some sale items. She had her back to him, but his presence drew her to him. "Mark? Hey, baby, I'm glad that I can finally have some of your precious time." He picked up on Alexis's sarcasm, but he chose not to feed into it. He understood her reasoning behind it. He knew that he'd been neglecting her as of late and her feelings were hurt. "Hey, sexy Lexy, you know that I always have time for you. Stop tripping."

Alexis looked at him with a "nigga, please" look on her face. "Look, Mark, I'm not tryna add any unnecessary stress to you, but we must talk." Mark peeped the seriousness in her body language and he heard it in her tone. "I feel that, Alexis. That's why I'm here. I know that you deserve explanations." Alexis turned to one of her assistants. "Margaret, I'll be back shortly. Hold the shop down 'til I return, girl."

Margaret had a twinkle in her eye. She automatically thought the boss was going for a nooner. The twosome strolled down to a restaurant on the Avenue of the Americas. "So Mark, what is it that you need to explain to me?"

Alexis's forwardness threw him off. She was in a no game playing mood and she wanted him to be aware of it. "Well, Alexis, it's like this. From the jump, you knew I was married. You yourself know that we didn't plan for us to go the route that we went. Granted we took it there, developed a beautiful thing." Alexis didn't interrupt. She just peered at Mark accusingly. "Anyway, I never promised you that I'd leave Kim. I was straight up with you from the giddy-up." Alexis just rolled her eyes and sighed. "I'm saying, Alexis, you know that me and Kim just had a baby girl. On the strength of that, we are trying to make our marriage work."

Alexis finally spoke. "So what you saying, Mark? What? You tryna get ghost on a sista'? Y'all niggas ain't shit! You knew my situation. You knew what time it was. I've discussed things with you that I've never discussed with anybody. Nobody! You know I haven't let anyone near my heart, let alone in it. You're the first, Mark. You're it! I love you, baby. Now you coming at me with this b.s.? Just say what you're trying to say."

Mark took a deep breath before responding. "I'm saying that we got to stop seeing each other, Lex. I mean, at least not on that level. We can't stay on the level we on." That caused Alexis to get indignant. "On what level? What level, Mark! Shit, it's all or nothing with me. What? We supposed to act like what we had never existed? I'm supposed to say okay, Mark, go patch things up with wifey? Fuck that! I'm supposed to be wifey, Mark. ME! I guess I'm supposed to just play my position, huh? What do you expect a sister to do? You think I'm gonna just sit around and wait and see? You think I'm gonna pause and put my life on hold for your ass? Nigga, you got life all fucked up! It ain't no 'we just friends' now. It ain't no 'we not on that level' now. Do you hear me, Mark? It's all or nothing with me. I'll be damned if you're leaving me too." Mark looked at Alexis like she had lost her mind. He'd never seen Alexis flip the script like that. He was viewing her in a new light. It was true that he did know about Alexis's past. He knew all about the sexual and mental abuse caused at the hands of her stepfather. He knew all about her lack of trust for men. Mark knew that she was vulnerable, yet he still chose to cross that line. His conscience began to plague him again, but he willed himself to stay the course.

"Yeah, I hear you, baby. Listen though, Essence deserves both parents in her life." Alexis replied, "You can and you will be in her life, Mark. You don't have to stay chained to your wife for that to happen. This is a new day. You can take care of Essence and be an active part in her life. You don't have to stay married to her mother for that to happen, baby. You told me you weren't happy in your marriage, remember that? You forgot that I'm the bitch holding you down. Oh, you forgot? You said that you were behind on bills and shit and that you wanted to get in the mix. What did I do, Mark? What did I do? I introduced you to Rondue, that's what. On the strength of you being my man, he plugged you in. I guess you forgot all that, huh? When you needed a thoroughbred ride or die chick, who filled that position, baby? Who fit the fuckin' bill?"

"Yeah, I ain't gonna front, Lex. All that you said are actual facts. You did that. And the things you said, I said. I said that. You know how I feel about you, ma. Ain't nothing gonna change, boo. But the shit still remains, Alexis. Like I said, me and Kim gonna try and work shit out. Now if what we had is real and meant to be, then it will be, Lex. You can't stop what's meant to be. You can delay it, or cause a minor setback, but you can't stop it. You know that old saying: if you love something - "

Alexis completed the cliché. "Let it go, and if it's meant to be, it'll come back to you? Yeah, I'm familiar with the saying. So what of it?" "Well, that's what's up, Alexis. I got to try for that little girl. I owe her at least that much. Essence deserves to have what I didn't. She deserves both parents - both of us. I can't have another man around Essence. These motherfuckers are sick out here. It's like they're controlled by these spirits of perversion."

By saying that, Mark played on Alexis's psychological issues. He knew that deep down the victim in her wouldn't argue with his logic. "I'm not going away, Mark. You wanted me, now you got me."

CHAPTER 7

Kim was still coming to terms with Mark's hustling ways. She was not accepting of the fact, but she was attempting to be more understanding to it. She began encouraging him more and she attempted to be more sympathetic to Mark's issues. Kim refused to get divorced like 85% of her friends. She had the drive and the willpower to see her marriage through. They set aside Saturdays as date days. Every Saturday they packed up Essence and sent her to Granny's house.

"Man, this line is long." They had decided to go dancing one Saturday. They were both looking good and feeling good. Mark had been admiring his wife all evening. "Baby, you're the baddest chick out this joint." Kim smiled and reveled in Mark's compliments. "You are looking really good to me, Kim." Mark's compliments weren't unfounded. If Kim wasn't the baddest, she was definitely in the forerunning.

The inside of Club Shadows was jam-packed. They were in the middle of an old school mix. "Ooh, baby, that's my jam!" Kim grabbed Mark's hands and rushed immediately to the dance floor. They hadn't danced together in a long time, but their chemistry was unmatched. They complimented each other in every way. All eyes were on them as they grooved to the throwback jams. The classic golden era music always seemed to spark nostalgia within them. They were oblivious to the attention. They were wrapped up in each other in their own world.

"Go baby, go baby, go! You still got it, Mark, do ya thang, boy!"
Deep in the cut and watching the scene unfold was Alexis. It was coincidental that they were in Club Shadows together.

Her girlfriend Claudia was tired of seeing Alexis in a funk. Earlier in the evening, she had told Alexis, "Come on, girl, you sitting around like a bump on a log." She was aware of Alexis and Mark's situation and she was determined to get her girl out and about. "We are going out, girl." They had been in the club for about fifteen minutes when Mark and Kim arrived.

"Shit," Alexis mumbled. "That must be his wife, Kim. I have never seen her before. She a'ight, but she ain't got nothing on me." Claudia turned to see what Alexis was speaking about. Deep inside, Claudia was always a little envious of Alexis, and secretly she somewhat enjoyed Alexis's dilemma. "Naw, she ain't got nothing on you, but girlfriend is a dime though. Oh, and she is rocking them shoes too." Alexis sucked her teeth at her friend's assessment. "They probably some Payless knock-offs."

Alexis attempted to ignore Mark and Kim, but like a magnet, her eyes were drawn to them. She witnessed the happiness and bliss that exuded from them. She couldn't take it anymore. As she watched them dance the night away, she slowly saw hers and Mark's chances of being together evaporate. "Claudia, girl, let's go. I'm tired of this scene already."

Claudia enjoyed seeing Alexis's discomfort. She felt as if this was the needed episode that would knock Alexis off her high horse. She was jealous of Alexis always having that air of togetherness. The unraveling that was brought upon Alexis satisfied her. "Girl, we just got here. Let's kick it for a little while longer" "Look, Claudia, girl, you can do you. If you want to stay, then stay. But like I said, I'm bouncing."

Claudia quickly weighed her options. She had ridden to the club with Alexis. She didn't want to have to put up with a buster just to get a ride home. From now on she vowed to start driving her own car. "All right, girl, let's go."

Mark and Kim continued to enjoy themselves at the club. Their union was getting stronger each and every day. Mark was still grinding in Tompkins, but all of the extracurricular activities he had nipped in the bud. Even though he missed Alexis, he was recommitted to his family.

They had spoken on the phone a few times, but Alexis gave Mark his space. She felt as though he would come to his senses eventually. Besides that, she considered herself top notch. She didn't want to appear to be needy or desperate. "Whoo, baby!" Kim said, out of breath. "My feet are killing me."

Mark laughed as he sat down. He gently placed her feet in his lap, removed her shoes, and massaged her feet. She looked at Mark with hungry eyes. "You ready to ride on out, love?" Mark asked as he drank a shot of Patron. "'Cause I'm saying, if you still want to get your boogie on, we can." Kim looked at her man with a look laced with longing. "Yeah, love. I want to get my boogie on, but not on the dance floor."

Kim's innuendo tickled Mark. "Girl, you are so nasty! I love when you talk down and dirty. Let's go" When they approached the car, they weren't prepared for the surprise that awaited them. "What the fuck!" exclaimed Mark. It was apparent that someone had taken Jazmine Sullivan's song literally. They had busted the windows out on his car. On the hood, carved in the metal flake paint, were the words "it ain't over".

"What's all this about, Mark?" Kim was fuming. Mark appeared to be baffled as well, but he knew exactly what was going on. "I don't know what's up, Kim. Somebody must've got the wrong whip." Kim got really nervous as she looked around. "Maybe it has something to do with your hustling. See, Mark? That life isn't safe. You can't keep living like this, baby. It's affecting us now." Kim had worked herself up to a slight hysteria. "What if they come to the house next? What about me and Essence? What have you gotten yourself into?" It hurt Mark to see his wife in this terrified state, but he couldn't tell her the truth. It would destroy their marriage. "Chill, Kim, let me think. I got to get a police report so I can get it to the claims adjuster. Just calm down, baby. We're going to be all right. I promise."

****

"Alexis, why you pull that fuckin' stunt the other night?" Alexis didn't even try to hide the fact that she went Freddie Kruger on Mark's car. "That's just to let you know that you playing games with the wrong one. You are playing with my heart and shit. Since you like playing so many games, we gonna play my game."

Mark was exhausted. "What fuckin' games you talking about, yo? I've been straight up with you from the beginning. You are bugging out, Alexis, for real." Alexis began yelling and screaming into the phone. "Listen, Alexis, if you think your actions are gonna bring us back together, then you're sadly mistaken. That shit you doing is definitely gonna keep us apart. It seems like you're trying to make me stay put where I am?"

Alexis saw the plot for what it was. "Save that shit, Mark. I saw you and wifey dancing the night away. I must've been a fool to fall in love with you. Y'all don't look like y'all in an estranged marriage to me. Y'all muh'fuckas all cuddled up and shit. Y'all look like y'all in love. What about me, Mark?

Mark just shook his head. He tried to be patient with Alexis. He tried his damnedest to understand her position. "Listen, Alexis, just don't let that foul shit happen again."

Alexis laughed. "Fool, you ain't seen foul yet, nigga. You took my love and pissed on it. You ain't any better than my step-pops. You're killing me slowly the same way he did." She hung up the phone before Mark could respond.

Mark slowly hung up the phone. *That girl got major issues*, he thought. *I must have been off my rocker fuckin' with her. I hope this little psychotic episode is over with. I ain't finna go through this bullshit. Why I got to get stuck with the crazy ones? First Kim bugs out, now Alexis. This bitch on some Jerry Springer shit. She ain't got no more times to flip out either.*

CHAPTER 8

"Look, Jackson, stop pussy-footing around. You owe us, ya fuckin' scumbag. Now we can throw your ass back in Rikers, or you can go make the buy. It doesn't make any fuckin' difference to us one way or the other." Marcus Jackson was between a rock and hard place. Detectives Zambrano and Silva had caught him dirty, and now they gave him the dirtiest ultimatum.

"All we need you to do is take this money, go score, and bring the goods back. Now what's it gonna be, Jackson?" Jackson was mad at himself for getting caught out there like that. He'd always considered himself a G. The current situation was a threat to that title though. "What the fuck you mean, Zambrano? You tryna turn me into a snitch, man. I ain't a fuckin rat."

The two detectives decided to play hard ball. They'd been partners for so long that they were always on the same page. "Ahh shit! What the fuck?" Jackson squealed as they cuffed him and threw him in the back of the undercover car. "What the fuck is y'all doing, man?"

Zambrano laughed. "Don't they teach you how to speak in school? 'What the fuck is y'all doin'?' You sound like a jackass, Jackson." Zambrano accelerated until they reached an abandoned house on Jefferson Avenue off of Bushwick. "Why the fuck we stopping here for, man?" Marcus was wracked with fear.

"Shut the fuck up, Jackson!" Silva pulled Marcus out of the back seat and dragged him into the abandoned house. The interior of the house was filthy. The local "rock stars" had turned the house into a smoking gallery. There were empty multicolored crack vials strewn all around the living room. The house reeked of urine, musk, and the overwhelming distinct smell of crack. The detectives beat Jackson until they were both gasping for air.

"All right, man, all right," Jackson pleaded. "I'll make the fuckin' buy, man. Just get the fuck up off me."

****

"Damn, Mark," Yosef was saying. "You catch on pretty fast, kid." Mark had been doing well managing the spot in Tompkins. He had definitely handled the business part well. As we all know in that particular business, though, gangster shit always followed suit. On the strength of Rondue, no drama ever reached Mark's doorsteps.

"It's time for you to build your own squad, duke. Me and my man can't stay here like this forever, bro. We got our own moves to make." Mark knew that this reality would eventually surface. "Yeah, I know, 'Sef. I sure hate it too, kid. Y'all some down-ass soldiers. I knew this shit was coming. It's been on a brotha's mind. I'm gonna holla at my homie P and see what the deal is."

"I suggest you do that ASAP, homie, because Rondue got some other shit lined up for us. This is our last night on." Mark grudgingly replied, "Yeah, I feel you, son. I understand y'all got to do what y'all got to. Real talk, I appreciate y'all brothas. That's on the one, 'Sef, for real." Yosef nodded his head in acknowledgment to Mark's props. "Yeah, baby boy, don't forget your arrangements with Rondue. Ain't nothing change, bro. You don't cop from nobody but us."

Yosef looked in Mark's eyes. "Oh yeah, one more thing: get your shit together." Mark looked puzzled. To answer Mark's curiosity, Yosef replied, "Hurry up and get your team together. There are some real wolves out here, bruh."

****

"I'm saying, P, I need you, bro. You know how we used to do it. I need somebody that I can trust. If I can't trust you, I can't trust anybody."

Paul looked at Mark like he'd lost his mind. "Mark, we like brothers, but I ain't tryna go backwards, man. That life ain't me no more. I mean, I ain't knockin' you for doin' you, but that ain't for me."

Mark looked horrified. "I can't believe this shit, P. Not you, kid. We been ride or die homies since day one. Now all of a sudden you ain't down no more?" Mark was thinking selfishly; therefore, reason wasn't an option for him. Paul's logic wasn't even being taken into consideration. "Man, let me find out that the homie P has got soft. I've seen it all now: my main man, P Dog. I never thought I'd see the day that you'd turn your back on me."

Paul just shook his head disgustedly. "Man, listen to yourself. What kind of nigga are you? You want me to slide back into that same pit that I came out of? That's dumb shit right there."

A little of Paul's logic began to seep into Mark's consciousness. Even though Paul had begun to make sense, Mark's predicament wouldn't allow it to take root. "Man, I ain't tryna hear that shit, P. I'm all fucked up in the game right now. My unemployment ran out two months ago, no more insurance, and to top it off, my savings dried up. You ain't feelin' me, P. I got to do what I got to do, fam. So tell me something good."

Paul looked at Mark with pity-filled eyes. "Yeah, I'm feelin' ya pain, Mark. I ain't know it was all like that, kid. Shit mad thick for you right now. Do what you feel is real, Mark. I can't get down though, homie."

Mark began to voice his dissatisfaction. "Hold up, Mark, chill, fam. My little cousin Malik might wanna get down. This type of hype is his M.O. anyway. This is what he's into. I'll link y'all up together." Malik was down to roll with Mark. He was a good fit. He was loyal, ruthless, and had recently fallen on hard times too. He and Mark vibed automatically.

****

"Y'all muthafuckas know what the fuck this is. Kiss the floor." Four armed, ski-masked men pushed past a customer and ran up in Mark's spot. "I'm telling you right now, if you even breathe too deep, I'ma body you." Only one man spoke. The other three took up positions in the trap. "We want the work, and we want the loot. If you wanna die for that shit, that's on you. Whatever jumps off, we leaving with it regardless."

Soldiers recognize soldiers. Therefore, three of the four guns were trained on Malik. Malik remained calm the whole time. The ski masks served to settle his nerves. If the gunmen had rushed the trap without ski masks on, then Malik would have been alarmed.

Mark, on the other hand, was shook. "Hold up, hold up, man." Mark pleaded for his life. "Ain't no need to pop off. All the work and the loot are right here." Mark practically had tears in his eyes. Once he saw the men relax a little, he decided to use what he thought was his trump card. "This shit doesn't belong to me though. This shit is Rondue's. Y'all fuckin' with Rondue's shit."

One of the masked men cold cocked Mark in the nose with the butt of his burner. "Fuck you, and fuck Rondue too, nigga." Mark grabbed his nose and rolled around on the floor. The three trained guns never left Malik. Malik, on the other hand, took in the whole scene. He thought to himself, *This nigga Mark is a pussy. His momma must've known what he was gonna be when he grew up. She had to; that's why she named him Mark. That's what he is, a fuckin' mark.* Malik never flinched. He tried to soak the whole scene into his memory bank.

The four men grabbed the goods and left as quickly as they came. Malik jumped up off the floor and ran to the window. Down in the courtyard he spotted four men getting away. Malik quickly grabbed the chopper from under the sofa and rained down the hot lead onto the fleeing men. The barrage of bullets never found their intended targets. Mark was still wallowing around on the ground. The gunfire snapped Mark out of his stupor. Mark was shaken to his very core.

****

Over the course of two weeks, Marcus Jackson had made several buys for detectives Zambrano and Silva. "All right, Jackson, you're on your way to freedom. You can crawl back under the rock you came from. We just need one more buy. After that you testify, then you go on with your pathetic life."

That caught Jackson off guard. "Testify? What?" he asked, baffled. "You ain't said a fuckin' thing about testifying. Y'all some dirty rotten muthafuckas." Both officers just laughed. "Shut the fuck up, Jackson. You know the game. You know how shit goes. Now get your nappy-headed two-bit ass in there and score."

Marcus didn't know how he had allowed himself to get in this position. He would be required to wear a snitch jacket for the rest of his life. He was absolutely disgusted with himself. "I can't believe this shit, man." Detective Zambrano sensed Jackson's reluctance. "Either that, or go back to washing draws on the Island."

****

Mark and Kim's relationship was improving vastly. They were communicating more, spending more time together, and as a result, their love life bounced back. She was still wrestling with the fact of his return to the streets, but she was dealing nonetheless.

When Mark came through the doors with a busted nose, Kim was immensely alarmed. Mark managed to placate her worry by assuring her that this rediscovered lifestyle was indeed temporary. Once again, she was dreaming about the ever elusive happily ever after.

****

"Damn, son. I see you makin' moves. You are workin' with these packs real swift like." Mark was serving Jackson a double up pack. "Yeah, kid, you know how shit is. I'm trying to get my feet up under me, you dig?" Mark decided to proposition Marcus. "Yeah, I can probably help you do just that, homie. Peep this. I got a spot on the team, man. Shit, we can put you on. You can do your thing up outta here. We can be 24/7 in this bitch. What you tryna do, bruh?"

That made Jackson feel even worse about his predicament. He had a shot at getting down with an up and coming team. Instead, he had reduced himself to the status of a rat bastard. He had to play his position though. "Damn, Mark, that's what's up, kid. Let me knock off this pack and think about it, then I'll hit you back." "A'ight, homie, but don't sleep. Shit doesn't stop, it pop, fam." Marcus left feeling like the sellout that he was.

****

"What the fuck?" Mark jumped up. He looked over and saw his terror-stricken wife. He wondered, *Who the fuck knocking on my door like that?* Kim had never fully recovered from the car being vandalized or from Mark's bloody nose. She was not cut out for the life Mark was living. She practically wet her panties visualizing a gang of thugs breaking into her home.

Mark jumped out of bed and rushed into the living room. He was hell-bent on protecting his family. "Who the fuck is it?" he yelled. "Open the door, Stevens. This is NYPD." *NYPD?* Mark thought. *What the hell is going on?*

Kim, hearing that it was the police, looked at Mark with questioning eyes. Before she could ask, Mark answered her question. "I don't know what the fuck they want, baby." There was another forceful knock at the door. "This is the last time. Mark Stevens, open the door, or we'll knock it down."

When Mark opened the door, a squadron of officers bum-rushed the house. They tackled him and cuffed him all in one fluid motion. The street indictment warranted a search of the home. Kim stood in shock as the officers tore up her house. She felt violated, naked, and bare. She attempted to comfort Essence as her world shattered around her.

"Mark Stevens, you are under arrest for the distribution of a controlled substance." As they took Mark out of the house, he locked eyes with his wife. He saw tears pouring out of his wife's distraught eyes. He wondered if his wife was strong enough to ride it out. He wondered if their fragile relationship was repaired enough to sustain this new blow. With his last glance he viewed his ladies, Kim and Essence, both crying like newborn babies. "Be strong, Kim. I love you, baby."

CHAPTER 9

Mark's final declaration of love served to reinforce Kim's dedication to their union. She not only wanted to prove something to Mark, she wanted to prove the same thing to herself. She wanted to prove that her time away at Serenity wasn't in vain. She wanted to show that despite her sheltered life, she could withstand adversity. She knew that she must tackle this obstacle unwaveringly and head on. She knew that she couldn't afford to duck, dodge, or ignore the reality of the situation. She chose to dig in her heels and declare her dedication to her man.

****

"Damn, Rondue," Yosef was saying. "That's a hard knock for Mark. It's one thing to get gaffled, but to back door it with a case? That nigga got all kinda bad luck." Rondue agreed with Yosef's sentiments. "Yeah, I feel you, 'Sef. The robbery was personal though. We got at him for the way he played my cousin. That there was sort of payback, yo. But I wouldn't wish getting knocked by 5-O on nobody, man."

"Yeah, I feel that, but what's even worse is if he decides to roll over on us? You know he ain't really built like us, Rondue. If they pressure son, is he gonna crack? We don't know if he a stand up dude or not." Rondue added, "Yeah, the thing is that he doesn't have a clue that we robbed him. At least he doesn't have any animosity or malice in his heart for us. As far as he knows, we ain't shown nothing but love."

Rondue didn't really want to rob Mark after putting him on and all, but it was GP. He didn't appreciate how Mark was playing Alexis out. When Alexis explained how Mark had done her wrong, Rondue was livid. Alexis was Rondue's heart. He loved her more than he did anyone else. She was all that he had left on this earth. Alexis made him promise not to hurt Mark physically, so he hurt his pockets instead. "Yeah, man. It's fucked up that ole boy caught a case, man. He was young in the game, but he was all right."

After further analyzing the situation, Rondue concluded, "He don't know enough about our set-up to hurt us. We gotta close down the spot in Tompkins, but everything else is a go. I don't think son gonna go out on us like that, but if he does, we'll be all right. Alexis loves this fool. I wonder how she's holding up."

****

Marcus Jackson had a change of heart in testifying against Mark. He chose not to go through with it because he wouldn't have been able to live with himself doing so. He got ghost at the last minute. Therefore, the district attorney had to squash the trial. Instead they came at Mark with a two-year plea bargain. Considering the time Mark was facing, he quickly signed the plea arrangement. He figured he could handle this amount of time. It wasn't like he was an innocent man, so considering this, he accepted his situation. *If Kim can just hold it together*, he thought, *we can withstand this. A minor setback for a major comeback.* He knew that she would be all right financially. It was her mental state that was suspect.

****

Elmira DOC. Elmira, NY

"Mail call." The C.O. began calling out mail. Every day Mark waited eagerly in anticipation of his name being called. Kim did not disappoint him. She was holding Mark down to the fullest. His commissary account was sitting fat, he received visits twice a month, she kept him laced with books, magazines, and pictures, and she wrote to him twice a week. Despite the circumstances, he was content.

"Mark Stevens," the C.O. called out. "Yeah, that's baby girl on the check in." Mark grabbed his letter and briefly inspected it. He peeped the handwriting and he didn't recognize it. There was no name in the sender's spot either. *Who the hell is this?* Mark thought. Curiosity got the best of him and he quickly snatched open the letter. His nose was assaulted by the perfume fragrance that was sprayed on the letter.

Dear Mark,

I hope this that this letter finds you in a good place despite the circumstances. In case you haven't figured it out yet, it's me, Alexis. Please don't throw this letter away without reading it. First, let me apologize. I admit that I spazzed out with your car. I childishly let my emotions consume me. That was the result of being hurt. That was the end result of me being scorned.

I should've carried myself a little better than that, but what's done is done. Truth be told, Mark, I'm still in love with you. I'm lost though. I don't understand this shit. For one, it's something that I've never experienced before. You know that I've never loved before, and you know why. This is where I am at a disadvantage. This first love shit is usually felt around high school. Here I am a grown-ass woman just now going through it. So yes, I admit that I handled things wrong.

Rondue informed me of your situation and I'm floored by it. I feel partially responsible because of the role I played. If you will, let me be a friend to you. Can you find it in your heart to do so? You must admit that we connected on a level that is higher than just the physical. This time apart has caused me to grow. My once cloudy understanding is now clear. I understand that before we can have any type of 'ship, the most important 'ship is a friendship. If you would allow me back into your life, I promise that I'll be more understanding. I will not ever broach the subject of you leaving your wife again. I won't broach the subject of us being anything more than friends. Most of all I miss your friendship. I genuinely miss you.

Mark was being pulled in.

I understand your position as well as your situation. All I want is how it was in the beginning, how it was before we crossed that line. Do you think we can go back there? Do you think we can begin anew? I assure you that you won't regret it. I won't let my love for you overtake me and drive me to selfish acts of obsession. Friends, I now understand, are the greatest possession in the world. Please, Mark, one way or the other, write back.

Love always,

Alexis

Mark refolded the letter, laid back on his bunk, and contemplated Alexis's offer of friendship. If he had to be honest with himself, he missed Alexis. In such a short time she had positioned herself in Mark's world. Under any other circumstances, he would have been with her, not to mention that the sex between the two was explosive.

Mark's cellmate, Domonique, sensed Mark's troubled state of being. "What's the dealie, Big Mark? I hope it's all good on the bricks." Cellmates were always on the lookout for their cellies getting bad news. It was common knowledge that nine times out of ten, bad news led to drama. This caused everyone to be on high alert. "Naw, everything cool, 'Nique. I just heard from a shorty that I ain't hear from in a minute." Mark proceeded to lace Domonique up about Alexis.

"Shit, home, you better jump on that. I understand you got a wifey and all, but a friend never hurts. You gots to have a backup plan, home. What if wifey decides she can't bid with you no more? And then you ass out, out there! At least if wifey do bounce - what's her name again,

Alexis? - that's right, Alexis can step in. Ain't nothing wrong with that, yo. I wish I would've had a plan B. I called myself keepin' it real with wifey. Shit, I didn't keep it real with my damn self. If I did, then I wouldn't be way upstate with nobody on the team. I'm telling you from experience, Mark, you need to cuff shorty too."

Mark thought about Kim's shaky emotional state. He had often wondered if she could withstand the test of time. He knew that she loved him, without a doubt, but he didn't know if the circumstances were too much pressure on her. "Yeah, I'm feelin' that, 'Nique. You just might be right, kid." "Damn right, I'm right. When you doing time, the more on the team, the better. Eventually they'll fall off one by one. Whoever left standing is the one, fam."

Mark opened up the doors of communication with Alexis. He relayed that they could retry friendship, but that she must stick to the script. Alexis agreed, but she had her own agenda. All she wanted was what she now had: her foot in the door. In her heart and mind she loved Mark. He was the first; if she had it her way, he would be the last.

CHAPTER 10

When Mark entered the visiting room and spotted Kim, he knew that something was amiss. She'd usually get up, run toward him, and rain kisses all over his face. On this day she simply sat at the table with her head bowed. She looked like a hopeless, defeated woman. *Man,* Mark thought, *she's starting to crack under pressure.*

Once Mark reached the table, he briefly stood over her. It took Kim a few seconds to realize that Mark was there. Upon realization she quickly jumped up and planted a passionless kiss on Mark's lips. Mark was troubled by her lack of enthusiasm. He decided to quickly address the issue.

"What's going on with you, baby girl? You looking down and out. Talk to me, luv."

Kim looked her husband in his searching eyes. He wasn't threatened or worried about Kim cheating on him. It was a minuscule possibility, but he was more concerned about Kim's mental health. He didn't want her to have a major setback due to him being incarcerated. He just wasn't sure how much she could withstand.

Kim sensed Mark's concern. She could see the worry in his eyes. "I don't know, baby. I'm just feelin' a li'l down, that's all." She could see the worry lines deepening in his face. "Don't worry, baby, I'm not relapsing or anything. I've still got my feet planted firmly up under me. It's just that I wasn't prepared for this. I mean, how can you, or do you, get prepared for this? I'm holding it together. I miss you so much though, bae. It usually hits me the hardest when it's late at night, when I'm lying in our bed and my mind starts to unload on me. That's my loneliest time. At night before I drift off to sleep, it's torture. You know during the day it's all work. In the evenings, little Miss Essence got me wrapped around her little fingers. That girl is something else too, baby. So I'm constantly on the go, but when it's time to unwind, my mind shifts to you…to us. I must admit that at times it's so painful. Just being apart from you is taking my spirits. I miss you so much, Mark. Sometimes I feel so lost. I need you, baby. I said I'd follow you anywhere and I will. I'm here, Mark, I'm not going away." Tears streamed down Kim's face.

Mark wondered if Kim was trying to convince him, or convince herself. He reached across the table to wipe Kim's fallen tears. "Baby, I know that the weight of this situation is real heavy on you. Every second of my waking day I regret putting you through this shit." Mark was telling the truth. He saw how much his actions were affecting his family and it was crushing. "I wish that I could rewind this, but I can't; that's not possible. This is a done deal.

Best believe though that once we jump this hurdle, we'll never have to jump it again. This is my promise to you, Kim. I know that it ain't easy, baby girl. I know you don't deserve this. This was no fault of yours. I appreciate you for holding me down too. It's almost over, baby. We done got through the hardest part already." Mark was in fear of losing Kim. "Just a little bit further, Mrs. Stevens. We're almost at the finish line, girl. But I hear you. I know that you're lonely, baby. Maybe you could find something that could help in that area. I remember you talking about joining a gym. What's up with that?"

Kim smiled through the tears. "What you tryna say, a sister getting chunky or something?"Mark looked at her incredulously before he realized that she was joking. "Hell naw, you ain't chunky, girl, you finer than a mutha! I wish that - "

She interrupted Mark's comments. "Don't start talkin' nasty, boy. That's the last thing I need to hear. Don't worry though, bae, we gonna make it through this. I'm gonna go ahead and join the 24 Hour Fitness off of the Van Wyck."

Mark readily agreed. "That's a good idea, girl. By the time you get to sleep you won't be thinking about shit else. You gonna be so tired after your day that you'll be out as soon as you hit the pillow top. With work, Essence, and the gym, you won't have time to be worrying. What time you gonna start going so I know when to call?"

Kim thought about it for a little before she answered. "Well, I don't wanna overload Mama with Essence. I need to pick her up by 6. I guess I'll go from 4 'til 5:45. I don't need too much."

Mark gave Kim the once-over and agreed. "You sure don't!" That caused her to blush, unleashing the beautiful smile that had been missing. They kissed and enjoyed the rest of the visit. Mark thought to himself, *We're gonna be alright. I think my lady can handle it. This shit is almost over. I hope she has the strength to hold me down.* Some of his fear and worry began to dissipate.

CHAPTER 11

Mark's thoughts about Kim joining a gym were right on point. The gym proved to be a void filler in Kim's life. With work, the addition of the gym, and Essence to consume her time, she thought less about her problematic situation and focused more on her present day consumptions. At the end of the day, she didn't have any extra energy to spend on things she couldn't control or change.

Meanwhile, Mark's prison time was passing by uneventfully. Unlike a lot of inmates, he didn't get caught up in the penitentiary games or the drama associated with being incarcerated. He mostly kept to himself, read books, and tried to get refocused. Outside of that he spent time on the yard working out. He chose not to jump into religion like some inmates do. He felt that most of them were playing games with God.

Alexis was bombarding him with a blitzkrieg style of an attack. Not only was she writing letters, she began sending risqué pictures and ultimately began visiting Mark. Once again she had her chess face on. She was not wearing any of Mark's defenses down. She was obliterating them.

Mark attempted to remind himself daily that his and Alexis's friendship was just that: a friendship. But he found it almost impossible not to think of her in a sexual nature. The risqué pictures that he received pushed him over the edge. Daily he found himself struggling and battling himself concerning Alexis. The thing was he wasn't sure if he was winning the battle or losing it.

****

Alexis went all out in preparation for her visit with Mark. She decided to book an appointment at the spa and beauty shop. She chose to pamper herself with the full treatment: hair, mani/pedi, massage, facial, the works. Alexis draped herself in a titillating dress, which was designed with the intentions of enthralling Mark completely. She clothed her skin in the most delicate of fragrances and adorned herself with just the right touch of jewelry.

When Mark entered the visiting room he was taken aback. He spotted Alexis immediately. Mark quickly scanned the scene and noticed that all eyes were on Alexis. People curiously watched to see who the lucky man was to be visited by such a jaw-dropping beauty. Alexis fit the cliché. She was most definitely a sight for sore eyes.

Upon seeing Mark, she slowly stood and allowed Mark to get a visual of her entire package. She set out to show him what he had been missing. Her effects did not go unobserved, for they met her desired effect. Mark rushed to her and embraced her like a desert-ridden soul embraces the hope of finding water.

They hugged and kissed until the visitation C.O. discouraged them with the typical "no touching" line. Mark inhaled Alexis's fragrance and tried to mesh his being with hers as they clung to each other.

"Be seated. This is your last warning." Mark kissed Alexis one last time, then they reluctantly sat down. A sucking of the teeth and rolling of the eyes was directed at the C.O. "Damn, Lex, you lookin' real good, ma." Alexis batted her eyes in what she figured to be her most demure look.

Mark got a kick out of this. "Let me find out you up in here tryna front like you the Virgin Mary when you know that you're Mary Magdalene." That broke the ice as the two chuckled. "Oh, you got jokes, huh? Don't front. I see the way you salivating over this," she said as she swirled her head in the typical hoodrat fashion.

"Yeah, I can't front, sexy Lexy, you got it." "I'll be right back, boo. Let me get you some snacks." Alexis could have gotten the snacks before Mark arrived, but being the master chessman that she was, she didn't. She wanted Mark to get a visual of her going as well. As she sashayed towards the vending machines, she paused and looked back over her shoulders. Busted!

Once again her actions met her desired effect. Mark was tuned in like brothas used to tune into the video music box in '85. The exception was that he wasn't watching Ralph McDaniels or Vic the Kid. Mark was strictly focused on Alexis. *Damn*, he thought, *Alexis looking real tasty.*

She returned to the table with what looked like everything the vending machine had to offer. "Here you go, boo." She peeped Mark eyeing her. "Why you looking like that?" Mark tried to regain his composure. After seeing hard heads and butch-like women all day, it was good to see such a beautiful creature. "Naw, it ain't nothing Alexis. So how you doing?"

They engaged in idle conversation over the course of the visit. "So Mark, how are you and wifey getting along?" The question threw Mark for a loop. He didn't know if Alexis was sincere, or if she was being sarcastic. He figured that she was more or less trying to see where his and Kim's relationship stood. "Everything is okay," Mark said unconvincingly.

Alexis sensed this and pounced on it. "Mark, baby, we're friends ain't we, boo? Well, friends talk to each other. You can talk to me, Mark. I'm here for you." Mark, tired of having his emotions bottled up, unloaded them on Alexis. During this one-sided conversation, Alexis soaked it all up. Mark even went on to tell Alexis of Kim joining the 24 Hour Fitness off the belt.

"Well, that's good advice, Mark. Just try to mellow out as best as you can. You won't be any good to anyone all stressed out. I wish that I could give you one of my happy ending massages. You remember my massages don't you, Mark?" As a reply, he smiled at the memory. "I know what you need, daddy. I wish I could take care of you." The direction of the conversation began to arouse Mark's lower nature. Before he could dive in too deep, the C.O. announced, "The visitation is now over."

Alexis gave Mark a knowing smirk. Mark, on the other hand, looked crushed. "Don't worry, daddy, I'll be back to see you. Until then I'll send you some pictures of mama. You need to start calling me too, boo. I'd like to hear your voice sometimes." Mark swallowed the lump in his throat. "Alright, Lex, I will."

They stood, embraced, and gave their farewell kisses. Alexis left, floating on cloud 9. She felt as if she was the victor. She felt as if she was corralling Mark's heart to her. The gloves were off. It was no holds barred. Alexis was willing to do everything within her power to win Mark. By hook or by crook, nothing was beneath her.

CHAPTER 12

Kim's breathing was so accelerated that she saw white dots before her eyes. She was so glad when the instructor yelled, "Time!" She couldn't wait to get off of the cross trainer bike. Kim had opted to take the spinning class three times a week. She was what you would consider a newbie, but she was really determined.

"Gurrl, I thought I was finna pass out." Kim had invited Stephanie along as her visitor. "I know, girl, I feel like a heifer in here amongst these anorexic divas." Kim knew the feeling. She was by no means a big woman, but around these hard bodies, she felt out of shape. "I know what you saying, girl. Somebody needs to take up a food drive for these people." They continued to joke as they toweled off.

"Okay, what now, Jane Fonda?" Stephanie teased. "Girl, bump you. If you can hang, it's time to hit the ab lab." The ab lab was a class that concentrated on all aspects of the abdominal muscle. It was a thirty-five minute class. "What you mean if I can hang? I can hang with the best of them. And you, Ms. Thang, are a New Jack."

Kim snickered. "Let's get it then. The class is getting ready to jump off." Fifteen minutes into the class Stephanie was off to the side complaining of muscle cramps. "Girl, I think I pulled something," Stephanie whined. Kim shushed her in embarrassment. She continued to perform the exercises that the instructor demonstrated. Stephanie was reduced to watching Kim.

This workout shit is for the birds, she thought. *Kim is doing her thing though.* After the workout the duo went to the gym's bar to order some energy smoothies. "Girl, you can have this workout shit."

Kim wasn't surprised at Stephanie. She knew that Stephanie wasn't the workout type, but she was hoping for a workout partner. "Girl, it's just day one, week one. How you gonna quit like that? The first day is always the hardest. Come on, Steph, you actin' all soft, girl."

Stephanie wasn't having any of it. "Listen, Kim, do you. I ain't with this. Besides, the men I know like 'em thick. I ain't tryna be sweatin' out my perm. This ain't me." A female that was sitting at the bar butted in. "She's right, girlfriend, the first day is brutal. After that, it gets easier."

Stephanie looked at her in a "who asked you?" way. Kim, on the other hand, was happy to have somebody on her side. "That's what I'm trying to tell her." Stephanie sucked her teeth. "Damn what y'all saying; it's a wrap! Find yourself a new workout partner." Kim and the lady laughed.

"I didn't mean to butt in. I just over heard y'all and I wanted to encourage you. My name is Simone, by the way," she said, extending her hand. "Stephanie," she said stiffly. "Please excuse her, Simone. My name is Kim. How you doing?" Kim asked as she extended her hand.

"Nice to meet you, Kim. I'm doing alright, girlfriend. Trying to get used to this working out routine. I feel what Stephanie was saying. I can definitely relate to it. It is indeed rough in the beginning. I have to stick it out though." Once again Stephanie sucked her teeth.

Kim rolled her eyes at Stephanie's attitude. "Yeah, I feel you, Simone. I gots to stick it out too. I thought it would be easier with a workout partner. As you can see though, my workout partner ain't into working out."

Simone chuckled at this. "Well, I'm usually here around this time if you wanna hook up. I can use a partner to push me too. Sometimes I may run out of gas and need a boost."

Kim was relieved to hear that. She felt that a good workout buddy was what she needed. "That's a bet, girl." Kim reached into her fanny pack and retrieved a card. "Here's my number, Simone. Call me."

Simone took the card. "Alright, that's cool. I'm just moving here from Atlanta. This could work out all the way around. I can get a workout partner and gain two friends in the process." Simone made sure to include Stephanie.

Stephanie brightened. "That just might work, girl. Ms. Thang here," she said, motioning towards Kim, "act like she can't hang no more. Maybe you can help me drag her out of the house sometimes." "That's a deal," Simone said. The threesome departed feeling hopeful - hopeful about different things, but hopeful nonetheless.

****

Over the course of a few weeks, Kim and Simone developed a bond. They were working out together during the week and occasionally getting together on the weekends. Stephanie was caught up with yet another man; therefore, she was scarce. Kim, missing the company of her sister-girl Stephanie, naturally gravitated toward Simone.

"Girl, ever since you hooked Stephanie up with your relative, she been M.I.A." Simone agreed by nodding her head. "I know, right? They acting lovey dovey. It's sickening." She laughed. They were sitting in the lounge of the gym drinking energy drinks. They were attempting to recuperate from their workout. "So, what's up with you, Kim?" Simone asked, pointing to Kim's wedding ring. "I mean, we been kicking it for a while now, right? Forgive me for my nosiness if I crossed a line. I mean, I see that big ole rock. I don't never hear you talk about your husband though."

Kim got quiet. Simone sensed Kim's reluctance to discuss her personal business.

"I once had a husband too, but he was killed by a drunk driver. That's why I had to get out of Atlanta. Everything that I saw reminded me of him. Old places that we've been together haunted me. I couldn't take it anymore. Everything down there reminded me of Trindell. He was Mr. Atlanta, girl. I was going through a nervous breakdown, Kim.

If I would have stayed, ain't no telling if I would have made it back. I withdrew from the world. I miss Trindell like crazy, but I learned to cope with it. The change of scenery has been good to me." Simone took a deep breath and wiped a tear from her eye. "Forgive me if I made you feel out of sorts, but I needed to unload that. I don't have very many people that I can talk to."

Kim responded. "No, girl, I understand." The two women were silent for moment. They were both wrapped up in their own thoughts. "Well, Simone, my situation is not as tragic as yours. I've lost my husband too, but it's only temporary. I lost him to the system. My Mark is incarcerated right now. It's been so hard without my man, but I now realize that it could've been worse. He was living a life that I wasn't aware of. His double life came back to claim him too." Kim managed to hold in the tears that were brimming beneath her eyelids.

"That's not too bad considering that your loss is not final. You two guys can work everything out and get back on track. Just hang in there, girlfriend. Don't give up on true love. I know I'm not," Simone added.

****

Stephanie was addicted to bad boys. Simone's relative Jack certainly fit the bill. "Hold me tight, girl!" he screamed back over the wind. They were racing down Fountain Avenue. They had easily surpassed speeds of 125 MPH. Jack was pushing his chromed-out 1200 to the max.

They finally slowed and pulled over at the top of the strip. There were several souped-up cars and motorcycles there. "We're here." Stephanie was confused. "What are we doing here?"

Jack looked at Stephanie like she was slow. "These boys out here racing for stacks, car titles, everything!" Stephanie looked horrified. "Hold up, Jack, you getting ready to race?" He saw her petrified look and laughed. "Naw, I ain't racin', girl. Who I look like, Evil Knievel or somebody? I came through to get my bet on. I came to show love to my man Peedi. Wait right here. I'll be right back."

****

"Come on in, Simone, make yourself comfortable." On that Saturday, the girls didn't feel like going out. They opted to chill at Kim's place, drink wine, and watch movies. "Girl, I appreciate you inviting me over. Lord knows I didn't feel like clubbing tonight. It's been a long week. This is a nice change of pace."

Simone walked into the spacious living room. She admired the decor. "You have a beautiful home, Kim." She walked over to a wall that displayed family pictures. "And you have a lovely family. You most definitely been blessed." At the sight of Kim's familial pictures, Simone got emotional. "Who knows, if Trindell didn't get killed, what could've been?"

Kim gave Simone a second alone. She went to kitchen to pour two glasses of Zinfandel. When she returned to the living room she found Simone composed. "Girl, don't let me rain on your parade. I'm so sorry that I cracked up like that. I don't know what got into me."

Kim gave Simone a sincere look. "Girl, don't sweat that; let that. It's not healthy to keep shit bottled up."The two proceeded to down the bottle of wine before polishing off another. They were feeling goofy. They decided to put on some music and dance around. They were listening to all the throwback jams. When Eric B and Rakim came on, Simone jumped up and started dong the Wop. Kim got a kick out of this. The next was a Biz Markie song. Kim got up and did her rendition of the Biz Markie dance. "Girl, you ain't doing that right," Simone complained. "You too stiff." She giggled.

"Well excuse me, Ms. Dancing with the Stars." Simone laughed. "You gots to swing your arms like this." Simone properly demonstrated the Biz Markie dance. When the Humpty Dance song came on, they both jumped up to do the Hump. At the end of the song, both women were out of breath.

"You're crazy, girl!" The spell of depression that had covered Simone earlier had been been lifted. "We're going to have to do this again sometime, shawty. This was really therapeutic for me." Kim agreed. She enjoyed Simone's company. "Yeah, that's a bet, girl. We'll do it soon." Simone started to gather herself. "You going to be alright getting home?" Kim asked.

"Girl, this wine got me on fire. I'm feeling so horny. I'm finna dial me up a booty call. I don't know about you, but Miss Kitty needs stroked every once in a while." Kim shook her head. "Girl, I know what you mean. I can't wait for Mark to get home." Simone looked at Kim in shock. "You mean too tell me that you ain't getting no maintenance? That box's gonna dry up, girl."

"Tell me about it," Kim replied. "Well, I gots to get me something long, black, and hard." That night marked the beginning of an exotic dream for Kim. Simone re-sparked the desire and wantonness in Kim. Kim had suppressed these desires in her attempts to wait for Mark. Now she was being tortured by her lifelike dreams. Simone had lit the match. Now Kim's small flame was an inferno.

CHAPTER 13

"Listen, Alexis, you just can't be poppin' up on a brother like this." Alexis looked crushed. "Well excuse me! I thought you'd be glad to see me." Like always, Alexis had taken special preparation in her appearance when visiting Mark.

"Come on now, Lex, I'm always happy to see you, ma. But that's neither here nor there. Don't start that shit. Now how you know I ain't have another visit scheduled for today? You know the situation. This type of shit can cause a major conflict. I thought that you was Kim visiting."

Alexis sucked her teeth. "Honey, you wish Kim looked this good." "That's not the point. The point is you are out of line." Alexis sulked and pouted like a child. "Well excuse me for caring, damn!" Alexis knew that when she drove upstate to Elmira she wasn't playing her position. Her take was that she was tired of playing a position and ready for an upgrade. Even though she was in love with Mark, she still had her pride. Alexis began gathering her things.

"Where you goin', Lex?" Alexis narrowed her gaze and sucked her teeth. "Please, Mark, I know when I'm not wanted. I'm getting ready to go!" "Go?" Mark said a little too loudly. "You trippin' now, Lex, for real. What you talkin' 'bout you getting ready to go? Sit down, girl. You ain't going nowhere 'til visitation is over with."

Alexis was perplexed, or she feigned to be. "I thought you said I was outta line. You said that your precious wife was coming." Mark replied with forced patience. Between clenched teeth, he said, "Alexis, sit down. Even if she was coming, it's too late now. I've already been marked off for a visit."

Alexis sat down with a look of triumph. "Well, mister, you need to lose the attitude. We might as well enjoy this time together. Next time I'll be sure to check in with you to get my orders," she said sarcastically. "Furthermore, what's done is done. Now come here and give mama a kiss." Mark shook his head disbelievingly. "Girl, you something else."

The remainder of the visit was pleasurable. "Visitation is over," the C.O. finally informed everyone. Mark and Alexis stood to embrace each other. "So, do we have an understanding, Ms. Thang?" Alexis tried to smile her most reassuring smile. "Yes, daddy. We have an understanding. I'll wait until you tell me to come. Just don't make me wait too long, boy. I just might have to bust you up outta here."

Mark chuckled. "As a matter of fact, you can start coming every other weekend." To confirm this, he stated, "So not next weekend, but the weekend after I'll see you." This tickled Alexis's fancy.

****

Kim, Stephanie, and Simone all got together to hang. The threesome rarely all got together at once. Stephanie was usually up under Jack (literally). "All of a sudden Ms. Busybody got time for us," Kim joked. "Girl, hush. Can't a sister get her groove on?" Stephanie replied.

"Hello!" Simone agreed as she gave Stephanie a high five. "Ain't nothing wrong with a little bump and grind," Simone teased. "Y'all so nasty," Kim chided. "Y'all know my boo is on lock. Y'all ain't got to rub it in, dang." Both Stephanie and Simone laughed. They could see that their girl was sexually frustrated.

"Girl..." Stephanie teased, "You need to let a plumber unclog them old rusty pipes."

At this, the ladies howled. Kim shot Stephanie the middle finger.

"Girl," Stephanie said, turning towards Simone. "Good lookin' out for the hook up with Jack. Whoo!" she said, fanning herself. "He's like a marathon man."

Simone scrunched up her face. "Too much information! Hello, he is my cousin, you know! I don't want to hear that nastiness." Stephanie laughed. "I'm talkin' all…night…long." The three women cackled like hens. The remainder of the night was like an adult slumber party. They drank, smoked a little herb, and listened to good music.

"We must do this again sometime," Stephanie said, preparing to leave. "Heifer, where you goin'? Where you rushing off to?" Stephanie smiled an all too knowing smile. "I'm going to see a man about a horse - or should I say, a horse part. God knows Jack is built like one."

"ILL!" Simone and Kim chorused. "See you later, Queen Vibrator." Stephanie ducked out of the door before Kim could throw anything back at her.

****

Over the course of a couple of days, Kim sank into a frustrated and melancholy state of mind. She was craving Mark desperately. The clock between her legs was ticking like a time bomb. Hanging around Stephanie and Simone shed light on her suppressed libido. Hearing about their escapades re-sparked Kim's desires. She began living her sexual life through them vicariously. Kim found herself on the phone with both Stephanie and Simone. They gossiped about their sex lives like school girls.

"I'm saying, Simone, I'm so sexually frustrated. It don't make no sense." "Shit, I don't know how you do it. I mean, I know you love your husband, but what he don't know can't hurt. You gotta do what you gotta do, girlfriend." That line of conversation had become an ongoing saga. "I can't go out on Mark like that, Simone. He's a good man, girl. I can't front though, I thought about it. But I can't give in to the temporaries of instant gratification. That shit can lead to a lifetime of pain." It seemed as if Kim was trying to convince herself of this instead of trying to convince Simone.

"Yeah, yeah, I hear you. Listen, I don't know what to tell you. You a grown-ass chick. I understand what you're going through though. I feel ya pain, girlfriend, trust me I do. But the reality of the situation is that you have to do what's best for Kim."

Kim sensed Simone's aggravation with her. "I hear you, Simone. Sometimes shit just gets a little overwhelming. I'll get it together, girlfriend. Well, let me get off this chatter box, chile. Essence is ready to eat now."

"Alright, Kim, keep it together, girl. It'll get better for you. Just put a little water on that fire." Both women rambled on a bit further, then said their goodbyes and rang off.

****

Kim went about her days trying not to be too consumed with the needs of her lower self. She wasn't successful in that regard though. She was able to maintain and manage during business hours. Once night fell, she was victimized by her desires. This night was of no exception. Kim tossed and turned in the middle of her bed in anguish. The doorbell rang to give her temporary relief of her reality.

"Who in the world is that?" It was the weekend, but Kim wasn't expecting any company. She planned to go to bed early so she could get up early to visit Mark. Looking through the peephole, she was shocked to see Simone. "Girl, what are you doing here?" Kim opened the door for Simone to enter.

"Nothing, girl, out and about. Just coming to check on you." Kim motioned toward the bag that Simone had. "What you got in that bag, girl? You're always shopping." Simone flashed a sinister smile. "Goodies, girl. Wake on up. Let's kick it for a little while." Simone was tired of hearing Kim complain about her nonexistent sex life. She intended to help alleviate Kim's woes. "Girl, go get some glasses. I got us some cognac to sip on."

Kim shook off her sleepiness and went to get the glasses. "Girl, I can only kick it for a little while. I gotta get up early to go see Mark." Simone smirked. "Alright, girlfriend, I just wanted to lift you spirits up a little bit." The two began drinking. The cognac was stronger than the type of drink Kim was accustomed to.

"Phew, Simone, this shit is hittin' hard." "Yeah, girl, I figured you needed something potent tonight. Let's smoke this joint. After that I want to show you some shit I bought you today." Simone secretly crushed up some Ecstasy pills into a fine powder. She then mixed the powder with the weed.

The combination of the cognac and the X-laced joint was overwhelming to Kim. "Damn, girl, I'm tingling all over." Kim giggled. "Yeah," Simone agreed, "I feel it too. It's getting hot in here."

Kim felt the same way. "Ain't it though?" Once again Kim felt the pulsating beat of her lower self. "Simone, make yourself comfortable. I gotta go to the restroom." Kim wanted to check her panties. She thought to herself, *I know my period didn't come early.* She checked only to find that her panties were soaked. They weren't wet with blood, but with her own natural juices. *What the hell?* she thought. *I'm hornier than a mug.*

When she came back from changing her panties, she found Simone clothed in only her bra and thong. "Girl, I hope you don't mind. It's hotter than a muthafucka in here." Kim was caught off guard, but she truly didn't mind. Being an athlete throughout school, she was comfortable around half-dressed women. "Naw, girl, it's all good. I told you to make yourself at home, didn't I?"

Simone turned to retrieve her shopping bags. As she turned, Kim's eyes were automatically drawn to Simone's bare rump. *Damn,* Kim thought, *Girlfriend's body is off the chain.* Like most women, Kim always admired other women's bodies. She had never acted on that admiration though. She chose only to acknowledge it.

Simone came back over to the couch. "Now girl, please don't be offended. I've been hearing your pain concerning your sexual activity. So don't be mad, but I took it upon myself to buy you some goodies." Kim was in the dark. "Goodies? What in the world you talking about, girl?"

Simone dove into the bag like a child on Christmas morning opening their presents. The first thing she emerged with was a strand of beads. Kim was perplexed. Next to come out of the bag was a vibrator. Kim was slightly embarrassed, but she was intrigued even more. "What in the world?"

Simone sensed Kim's uneasiness. "Just chill, girl, I got you." Simone finally finished unloading her taboo treasures. The table was filled with an assortment of goodies. It included a regular vibrator, a bullet, a butt plug, anal beads, nipple clamps, a dildo, a vibrator with a clitoris stimulator, and a few more toys. Kim just looked at the toys as if they were foreign matter. She wanted to curse Simone out for violating her personal space, but her desires forbade her to do so.

"So what do you think?" Kim looked blankly at Simone through blinking eyes. Finally she said, "Simone, believe it or not, I've lived a pretty sheltered life. I'm not experienced in this department. I mean, before Mark I wasn't a virgin, but I was damn near close." Simone looked at Kim like she was crazy. "What's that gotta do with this?" Simone asked.

"It means I don't know what to do with most of this shit." Now Simone looked at Kim as if she was foreign matter. "You gotta be kidding me, girl!" Simone sensed Kim's growing anxiety over the toys. "Look," Simone said, "let's smoke this joint, and after that I'll walk you through the steps of each toy." Simone produced another laced joint.

After they smoked it, both Simone and Kim were percolating. Kim experienced a heightened sexual energy that she'd never experienced before. She was at the realm of a whole 'nother galaxy - a galaxy inhabited by freaks controlled by their hedonistic urges. Kim squirmed in her seat, trying to tame the sexual beast with in her.

"Alright, listen, this right here is a vibrator with a clitoral stimulator." Simone went on to explain each toy and its proper use. Kim was clearly baffled. She had a multitude of questions. "How will I know if I'm doing it right?" she asked. Simone let out a dramatic sigh. The Ecstasy was cruising through her being as well. "Just go sit over there and watch."

Simone pulled the coffee table off to the side. She cleared a space for herself in the middle of the living room floor. She looked over the vast array of goodies and selected the vibrator with the clitoral stimulator. After careful consideration, she also selected a butt plug. The X pills had her so juiced up that she didn't need any other form of lubrication.

She looked Kim right in the eyes. "Alright, Kim, pay attention and learn. Don't think that I'm an exhibitionist and shit. I'm just trying to get you right, girl." Like Simone, Kim was juiced up as well. She was already in the zone. She was on edge and eager to watch Simone's instructional display.

Simone stepped out of her bra and thong. She stood before Kim in all of her glorious splendor. Kim's eyes traveled down south to find that Simone sported a fresh Brazilian wax. Simone's scent quickly perfumed the room. Kim noticed that her heart was beating fast, but for the life of her she didn't know why. Simone clicked the vibrator on. It emitted a low hum. "This has three speeds. It's best to start low, and as the orgasmic pressure builds, increase the speed."

Simone laid her bare apple bottom down on the luxurious carpet. She reached down with her hand and lubricated her anus with her own natural juices. Once this was accomplished, she inserted the plug. This caused Simone to let out a low, primitive growl.

The Ecstasy held her in a vice grip. She spread her vulva, exposing her clitoris. The "man in the boat" was front and center. She inserted the vibrator and lined up the stimulator with "the man in the boat". This gave a new meaning to rock the boat. Per the instructions she gave Kim concerning the speed, Simone followed suit. She started off low. Simone never broke eye contact with Kim. Their eyes were having a conversation all their own.

Simone began to moan as the vibrator was clicked to the next speed. She began to gyrate her hips rhythmically. The muscles in her anus began to grip the plug as they contracted. Simone was working herself into a frenzy. She reached for a nipple clip and clamped it onto her elongated nipples.

Simone began to buck against the vibrator with a sense of abandon. Kim's vagina began to twitch with anticipation. She continued watching Simone shamelessly and openly. With their eyes locked, she could see the passion dancing behind Simone's irises. When Simone clicked the vibrator to its highest level, she cried out in pure bliss. Her orgasm was building to its final crescendo. The hot waves racked her entire body.

Kim was captivated by Simone's freely driven sexual expression. She'd read about such liberated women, but until now, she'd never known one. Unconsciously, she began to rub herself. When Simone saw this, it pushed her over the edge. With a pop she discharged the butt plug. The contractions of her orgasm were that intense. She cried out in ecstasy. Her breath was coming in short, labored bursts. She finally broke eye contact by closing her eyes to ride the final wave to paradise. When Simone finally reopened her eyes, Kim was standing over her. She blinked her eyes to refocus. Kim was standing in front of her fully nude. This time Simone's eyes were drawn down south. Kim sported a freshly cut and trimmed triangle. She also noticed Kim's athletic, yet curvy build. Kim was fine!

In a husky, passion-filled voice, Kim said, "Do me. It's my turn now". When it was all said and done, Kim completely ravaged Simone. All of Kim's pent up passions, desires, and restraints, were let loose on Simone. Kim was shocked herself, but she relinquished control to her neglected lower self. She'd never participated in a lesbian act, but the X-laced joints goaded her to feel that it was a natural act.

They both returned to Kim's bedroom after the episode to retire for the night. When Kim woke up the next morning, she was in a hazy fog. The bed next to her was empty, but Simone's scent still remained. She was left to wonder if she had another one of her erotic dreams or if she had indeed experience a night filled with passion.

When she reached the living room, the evidence of the previous night's escapade was found. Her mind began to flash to vivid pictures of her naughty events. At the memories, her body tingled all over. Kim was on fire! This feeling, although it was delicious, plagued her. She was completely confused. She now questioned her sexuality. This forbidden act caused her to wrestle with her perceptions of morality.

When Kim went to the bathroom to shower, she was stopped in her tracks by the writing on the wall, so to speak. Simone had left a message on the vanity's mirror written in lipstick.

It read: *Kim, I don't know what got into us last night. I don't know if it was the alcohol, or maybe it was the weed. Whatever the case, it was a mistake. I've never got down like that before. I'm strictly dickly and I'd like to keep it that way.*

This floored Kim. She wasn't quite sure how she was feeling. She had come on to Simone, but in the end, it was consensual. When she thought about it, she felt like Simone had seduced her. Her normal sense of logic and reasoning was blanketed by her passion and lack thereof. Kim finally admitted to herself that she was turned out. She enjoyed the affair and she wanted to sample it further. Now it seemed like Simone was flaking out.

Kim finally gathered herself. She almost completely forgot about visiting Mark. When she arrived upstate, she was very late. Over the course of the short visit, she was distracted by flashes of Simone.

Mark could tell that something wasn't right with Kim. Needless to say the visit wasn't pleasurable for either of them. This marked the beginning of their own drama-filled soap opera.

CHAPTER 14

When Mark entered the visitation room, Alexis was on display, as usual. Lately, Mark and Kim's relationship was tanking quickly. The letters had slowed, the visits were unproductive, and the communication was strained. Mark suspected Kim of cheating, but you know what they say about assuming. Therefore, he tried to remain optimistic.

"Hey daddy," Alexis greeted him seductively. "What's good, baby?" Mark and Alexis's relationship, on the other hand, was building momentum. Alexis was on top of her game when it came to Mark. The visits were like clockwork, his commissary account was all love, and the phone calls and mail were up to par. She was proving to be a trooper. She showed herself to be down and in it for the long haul.

The conversations that they engaged in were far from trivial. They often expressed their hopes, ambitions, and dreams. At times they dove into their past. Other times they prophesied about their future.

"Mark, baby, I have something that I need to ask you." Mark picked up on the seriousness in Alexis's tone. He figured that she was going to bring up her status again. "Yeah, Lex, what's the deal? Don't go gettin' stiff on me now, girl." "I want to ask you some personal shit about you and Kim." Mark relaxed a tad bit. "Yeah, what you need to know?" Alexis rarely brought Kim up. Mark was curious as to why Alexis was doing so now. "Mark, are y'all on solid ground? I mean, how are y'all doing as a couple?"

Mark figured that Alexis was inquiring so that she could see if the two of them had a future together. "Why are you askin' me that, Lex?"

Alexis's response surprised Mark. "Because I can tell something is going on with you, boo. I mean, you seem happy when I see you, but just under the surface I can sense that something is wrong. Something ain't right with you, baby."

Mark wasn't expecting this. He had bottled up his suspicions about Kim. His thoughts of her cheating were causing a pressure that was unbearable. Against his better judgment, he decided to discuss things with Alexis. He knew that this violated rule #1 in the mistress's handbook: never discuss the wife with your mistress. But he needed to get it off his chest.

"So you think you know the kid like that, huh? We that connected where you can pick up when something ain't right?" Alexis sucked her teeth. "Stop playing, Mark. Boy, you know that you're my world. So what's wrong?" Mark chuckled. "Baby girl, you hit the nail on the head with that one. I don't know what's going on with Kim. I can tell you that shit ain't right though."

This was exactly what Alexis wanted to hear, but she had to appear sympathetic. "What makes you say that, boo?" "Well for one thing, she's been missing a lot of visits lately. Our communication is basically nonexistent. I get pictures of Essence every once in a while, but that is it. When we do finally speak on the phone, the conversations seem forced. Truth of the matter is that I think she's cheating on me."

Alexis was beside herself with joy. She restrained herself from exhibiting the elation that she felt. "Damn, boo, I know that it's already rough on you being locked up. I hate that you have this added stress on you. It does sound like she has something going on though. Is there anything that I can do for you?"

Mark thought about Alexis's proposal. He considered getting Alexis to take pictures of Kim and her new man. He quickly nixed that idea. "Naw, girl. Just keep doin what'chu doin'. If it wasn't for you, I'd be out of there." "I told you that I was your ride or die mama. Just don't you forget that, Mark. I'm always here for you, boo. You'll see. When it's all said and done, I'll be the last woman standing."

Mark was beginning to buy into this. Talk was one thing, but Alexis was showing and proving that she was down for him. When he came to think of it, she was down since day one. "Yeah, Alexis, I feel you. As each day passes by, I'm starting to think you're right." Alexis sneered, "Damn right I'm right! Don't sweat it though, boo, mama got you. Trust and believe that I ain't going nowhere either. I'll be here forever and a day. You can stake your life on that." Alexis's actions and determinations were winning Mark over. She was slowly but surely reclaiming pieces of his heart.

****

After Kim and Simone's sexcapade, Kim spiraled down into a vortex of confusion. She was deeply troubled about her craving and yearning for another woman. Her sexuality was in question. She now reconsidered he feelings toward her husband. She'd developed a seething anger toward Mark about his double lifestyle. She felt that if Mark could lie and hide one thing, then he could lie and hide two things. She began to view him in a different light. She now felt as if her life was a lie.

Kim, in her questioning state, decided to give into her desires. She began to pursue Simone romantically and with gusto. The sensations and fire that Simone set free in her were overwhelming. She lost hold of all reason and was claimed by passion. Simone had pushed buttons in her that had never been pushed before. Kim didn't even know they existed. Simone brought about sensations that Kim didn't know she could feel. Kim was yearning to feel them again. She was willing, even if it was brought about by the hands of another woman.

****

Simone had an unusually long day at work. The night matched her mood. It was dark, raining, and cold. As she strode up her walkway, a dark figure emerged from behind a tree. Fear's grip paralyzed Simone. She was frozen stiff. Her brain triggered her to run, but her body couldn't cooperate. She did, however, manage to let out a piercing scream before the dark-clothed stranger was upon her.

"Girl, stop all that hollering. If you don't want to see me that bad, I'll leave. You don't have to cause a scene." Kim had been calling Simone, but Simone had been dodging her. Kim felt that it was time to confront Simone with her feelings. She had caught Simone off guard.

Simone had to take a deep breath and calm down before the fear passed. "Kim, damn, you scared the piss out of me. What you sneakin' up on a sister for? It's like you stalking me, damn!" "I wouldn't have to sneak up on you if you wasn't ducking me."

Simone shook her head to clear the remnants of fear. "Girl, come on in." Simone passed by Kim and entered the house. Kim was determined to be heard. She'd pre-programmed herself not to leave until she got what she wanted. Ordinarily Kim wasn't the aggressive type, but something fierce had been unleashed in her.

Simone led Kim into the living room. "Make yourself comfortable. Let me go get out of these work clothes." "Alright, girl. Sorry to barge all up in your space, but we need to talk." Kim went to the mini bar and prepared herself a drink. Her nerves were frazzled. She was still wrestling with the moralism or adultery and lesbianism. This was too far outside of her normal comfort zone and Kim didn't know how to proceed. Once again she thought about turning back, but her passion prevailed.

Kim was deep in thought when Simone reappeared in the living room. Simone could see that Kim was conflicted. "A'ight, Kim, what's up?"

Kim was startled at Simone's brisk entrance. She took a final sip of her cocktail to ease her nerves. "You're what's up, Simone." Simone expected this. "Look, Kim, did you get the message I left on the mirror?"

Kim sighed. "How could I have not gotten the message? It was obvious, loud, and clear. I also received the other message that was loud and clear." Simone raised her brow in a puzzled manner. "What other message?" she asked. "The message that I received from your body," Kim answered. "The message that verified that our souls connected. Don't front, Simone, you know you felt it too!"

"I can't front, Kim, I felt something, but - " "No buts, Simone. I mean, this shit is taboo. It's new to me too. I've never gotten down like this before. I told you that I was sheltered. Besides, I've never had an affair on my husband. I'm still reeling behind this, but at the same time, I can't regret what I feel. You not only do something *to* me, you do something *for* me. I don't expect us to be all out in the open with it. I'm not trying to have some coming out party. We can be discreet without that shit, but I want you, Simone. Regardless of what your mouth says, I know you want me too. I see the way that you be looking at me. I've noticed it, but I never paid much attention to it though. Now you have my full and undivided attention. The question is, can I have yours?"

That threw Simone for a loop. "I don't know what to say. I mean yeah, you're right. I have viewed you in that light too. You're a beautiful woman. But I've never experienced feelings like this towards another woman either." Simone shook her head. "This is some scary shit. I've been purposely staying away from you. When I'm around you, I feel electricity. It's not supposed to be this way. Does this mean that I'm a lesbo?" That caused Kim to giggle. "Look, girl, I don't know what it means. What I do know is that we don't have to stop. We can do what we feel is real. Like I said, we can be discreet. Nobody has to know but us. We can carry on the outside like we been doing."

"What about your husband?" Simone asked. "I know, I've thought about that too. Like I said, I never cheated on Mark. I found out that before Mark got locked up, he was living a double life. I'm quite sure he was cheating on me too. Anyway, I'll cross that bridge when we get to it. That has no bearing on us. Let's do us."

Simone thought about this gently for a while. "I can't front, girl, that lovemaking was the bomb. Alright, Kim, but we have to keep this strictly between us. I'm not comfortable yet with this. In front of everyone else, we must appear to be the same as we were before."

"I feel you, Simone. I don't want to be outted like that either. I don't consider myself a dyke. This may be a little phase or something. I've read that 58% of women have experienced same sex relations before. In most cases it's in college though. It just something about you though, Simone."

They both hugged and agreed to continue seeing each other in that capacity. Their sexcapades were driven by an untamed passion. For Simone it was strictly a release, but Kim began to get hooked. She began to get attached emotionally. Transmissions were crossed and she began to develop feelings for Simone.

CHAPTER 15

Mark was preparing himself to return to the free world. He grudgingly accepted the fact that his marriage had fallen apart. Mark knew that he had a lot of things to repair and he accepted his responsibility. He decided with finality to leave the street life alone. Mark chose to pursue his electrical career once again. He knew that the streets not only contributed to, but were the major factor in his downfall. He had no choice but to realistically attribute the streets to his current predicament.

Over the course of time, Kim grew distant. His once loving and doting wife was now cold and indifferent. When they communicated, which wasn't often, she accused Mark of past infidelity. She relayed that Mark's lying and deception had festered into hate within her. In her mind, love had walked out the door and pain walked in.

Mark often asked if she was now using that frame of thought as an excuse and motivation to cheat. Kim always denied cheating, but Mark knew that she was lying. He could feel his wife slipping away. He was still willing to give his marriage another shot, though he was reserved. He thought that once he was free, he could fix things. *Besides*, he thought, *at least I'll still be in the house with her.* Mark still had one foot in the door.

Mark and Alexis's relationship, on the other hand, was still growing. He'd developed a sincere love for her. She satisfied her position with each and every visit. With each piece of mail and every accepted phone call, she established her worth. Gradually she began to feel Mark's love toward her grow. When Alexis gazed into his eyes, his lust was replaced with love.

Alexis began preparing for Mark's return home also. She knew that he was moving back into his soon-to-be ex-wife's house. She suspected that he had some loose ends to tie up. She wasn't trying to force him to move or push the envelope. Alexis had been patient this long and she continued to be. She knew that it was just a matter of time before Mark would be running to her.

Alexis felt the scales tipping her way. She reveled in the fact that she would be able to claim Mark totally.

Everyone was preparing in their own way for Mark's return home. Each person - Mark, Kim, and Alexis - had their own plans though. No one knew what the exact outcome would be, but each prayed that it would go his or her way.

CHAPTER 16

The flame was slowly burning out in Kim and Simone's illicit affair. Kim was a slave driven by her passions whereas Simone was just going through the motions. Simone began to get missing in action a lot more as of late. Kim was a wreck and torn up emotionally. She still chose to deceive Mark. She hadn't told him about her newfound lifestyle. She was wracked with fear, slight shame, and an overall feeling of guilt.

"Listen, Kim, I see that you going through it, girl." Simone had come up with the perfect way to slide back from their relationship. She decided to use the camouflage of concern. "I can tell that you're wrestling with something and I think I know what it is." She paused for dramatic effect. "I know that your husband is due to come home. Our thing has been rocky lately, and I'm sure that it has to do with him. I know that you have to go back to your picket fence, fairytale life." Kim began to protest, but Simone stopped her. "It's probably the best thing for Essence though. I mean, how long can we keep up this façade? How would you explain this to her?"

Just the mention of Essence broke Kim down. The reality of that fact always existed in the background. Tears began to flow down Kim's face. "I ain't trippin' though, Kim. I know that on the strength of your little girl, you have to do what you gotta do. I expect that as a mother you have a greater responsibility. I know that Essence comes first." Simone had expertly put the ball in Kim's court.

"I'm so sorry, Simone," Kim sobbed. "Thank you for being so understanding. Trust me, love, you were more than some little fling. You are more to me than a substitute for Mark. I'm really feeling you, Simone. You're right though, Essence deserves both parents in her life. So what do you propose we do about us?" Kim was faintly hoping that she could have her cake and eat it too.

"Girl, we still cool. Good thing we still in the closet," Simone joked. "We don't owe the public nothing. We can continue our friendship, boo. Who knows?" Simone teased. "We maybe could still even be friends with benefits."

This slight silver of hope satisfied Kim immensely. "You're something else, Simone. Girl, you're too much. Thank you for being so supportive and understanding." Simone wasn't too worried about losing Kim. She knew that Kim was lying to herself. Simone knew that she had captured Kim's heart through erotic means. "Just see where you and your husband stand. I'll be in the background, patiently waiting."

****

"Well, this is our last visit in here, Mark." Alexis had ridden out Mark's bid like a bonafide cowgirl. She played the part that unfortunately only a small percentage play. Mark knew Alexis was a rare breed. He'd come across many men that were incarcerated that weren't as fortunate, men that were married for years and were left for dead in a matter of weeks. It was like women were waiting for it to happen so they could be free. Some men had spoiled their women rotten and couldn't even get a penny from the very same women. Brothers didn't even know where their children resided, let alone how they were doing. Mark recognized Alexis's love for him too and he was reluctant to part with it. She deserved more. Alexis held him down better than his own wife did.

"Yeah, baby, this is our last visit in this hell hole. The next time you see the kid, I'll be a free man." Alexis turned inward within herself and zoned out. After a few moments, Mark realized something was wrong. "What's wrong with you, Lex? Why you getting all down? You should be happy that I'm coming home. Why you lookin' like that for?"

"Why I'm looking like this for? It ain't like you really coming home to me anyway. It ain't like we gonna be up under the same roof together, are we? Shit, it should be me though. It should be us. Did your wife carry you like I did? Hell no! It's like I did all of the work and she's reaping all of the benefits. You got me feeling like a chump right about now." Alexis shed a few tears for added effect.

Her little performance knocked the wind out of Mark's sails. Everything that Alexis said was totally true. She had gone above and beyond the duty of holding Mark down. The more that Mark reflected on the lack of support from Kim, the more he was tempted to start anew with Alexis. The only thing that hindered him from doing so was Essence.

"Hold ya head up, ma. Lex, stop crying and listen to me." Mark lifted Alexis's head up with tender care. "I feel you, ma. What you sayin' is some real shit. I'm feelin' that. Trust me, if Essence wasn't the issue, I wouldn't be going back down that road. You're right. You've proven to be the woman that's for me. I got to try though, for Essence's sake. Let me make this promise though, boo. It's already a rocky road with Kim, but like I said, Essence deserves a real chance. If it can't be worked out, I won't force it. I will have to help raise Essence the best I can from outside the house. After that point, if you still have me, then you got all of me."

Alexis brightened on the inside, but she didn't show this to Mark. "What about until then, Mark? Am I supposed to be okay with being put on the shelf? Am I supposed to continually put my life on hold for you?" Alexis broke down crying again. She was playing the theatric role to the tee.Mark felt bad about Alexis's situation, but he refused to not give Essence 100%. "I guess I am being selfish, Lex. I don't want nobody else to have you. I want you all to myself, boo."

"So what are you sayin', Mark? You want your cake and you want to eat it too, huh?"

"Naw, Lex, I know better than that. I just don't want to lose you."

"Let's just see what tomorrow brings. I can't front. You already know that I love you. Silly as it sounds, I know that you love me too. I understand about Essence though, baby. That's one of the things that I love about you too. I see that dedication in you. She is lucky to have you as her daddy. I must be honest; I'm a tad bit selfish. I hope that yours and Kim's relationship comes to an end. I know that you can be a full-time dad to Essence without being with her mother."

Mark nodded his head. "Like you said, Lex, let's see what tomorrow brings. Until then, where do we stand?" Alexis shook her head sorrowfully. "You know where we stand, Mark. You can't just turn love on and off. I don't work like that. Just have the decency not to play games. Don't string me along or sell me dreams." "You got that, boo. No games."

CHAPTER 17

Mark's re-integration process into society was going smoothly. He rejoined the electrician's union and they provided him with steady work. Once again he was doing the work that he loved and getting paid handsomely for it. His and Essence's bond was like magic. She was definitely a Daddy's girl. She wouldn't let Mark out of her sight.

Mark and Kim's relationship was another story. Kim's once communicative nature was reduced to a need to know basis only. Their sex life was basically nonexistent. Mark constantly found himself contemplating divorce.

"Kim, what's the deal with you? The vibe I'm receiving from you is ice cold. It feels like you don't want me here or something. You got to tell me something. What's up? For Essence's sake, we got to try and get out shit together. Come here, baby." Mark attempted to embrace Kim.

"No, Mark, stop. Don't touch me. I don't feel like it"

****

"Girl, we ain't kicked it like this in a while." Kim, Simone, and Stephanie had decided to get together for a girls' night out. For some reason the entire night, Stephanie felt like a third wheel. She couldn't quite place her finger on it, but she curiously watched Kim and Simone. She gathered that their bond must've grown while she was M.I.A. with Jack. They all rode together in Kim's new Infiniti SUV to City Island. After chowing down on some delectable seafood, they ventured out to BB King's club. The singer Kem was scheduled for a performance.

"Girl, hurry up! I don't want to miss Kem sing my jam." Stephanie commenced to singing. "Nowhere to hide when love calls, love calls your name, babe." They all laughed. "Don't quit your day job Steph," Kim joked. They arrived at BB King's just as Kem took the stage. The show was billed as a ladies only show. All of the waiters and bartenders wore black Chippendales.

"Ohh, girl," Stephanie said, fanning herself. "It's hot up in here. These brothers done took off their clothes." Kim giggled. "Girl, sit your fast tail down." Kim cut her eyes at Simone, "You too, Simone, sit down." Simone sucked her teeth. "Y'all act like y'all got some sense."

Simone sucked her teeth again. "Well excuse me, Miss prim and proper." Kim rolled her neck. "I got your prim and proper." During the performance, Kim sat there in a funk. Stephanie and Simone, on the other hand, were the life of the party. Kem serenaded both Simone and Stephanie. The women were swooning throughout Kem's performance.

"Girl, that show was the bomb!" Stephanie exclaimed. "It sure was," Simone agreed. "We need to do this more often. I really enjoyed myself tonight, y'all." Kim remained tight-lipped like a spoiled brat. "Anyway…" both Simone and Stephanie chorused. They both laughed and ignored Kim.

"It was good seeing you, Simone," said Stephanie. Kim decided to drop Stephanie off first. "Kim, girl, I'll call you tomorrow. We need to talk, girlfriend. I don't know what got your panties in a bunch, but it's not a good look." "Okaaayyyy," Simone co-signed. "Whatever, Steph. I'll talk to you later." Kim pulled off before Stephanie made it into the house.

"What's your problem tonight, Kim? You been trippin' for no reason all night." "You're the problem!" Kim screamed. "I seen you throwing yourself at those waiters, and that singer too. I'm sitting right there, and you're disrespecting me like that." Simone looked at Kim like she was kidding. "Are you serious? You can't be serious, Kim. This has got to be some fuckin' joke. What in the hell is really up? And miss me with that jealous act." Kim broke down crying. She sobbed, "Girl, I'm so sorry. I don't know what's up. It feels like I'm being pulled in a million directions. Mark is trying hard to fix our marriage. I feel an obligation for Essence's sake too. I can't deny myself though. I can't front, Simone. My passion lies with you. I'm a mess, girl." Kim blew her nose, and then continued. "I'm not blind, Simone. I can see, and I feel you moving on. This last month felt like you weren't into me anymore. I'm not stupid, girl. I know you must have somebody else. I'm not blind, nor am I stupid. So what's up? What's really going on?"

Kim was right. Over the last month, Simone had been spending time elsewhere. She no longer went to the gym and she barely spoke to Kim. "I don't know what to say. I've just been doing me. No big deal. You don't have to put on this big production. I mean, your husband is home, right? What do you expect me to do? Just hang around and see what happens?"

"I'm so sick of this!" Kim yelled. "Y'all are gonna give me a nervous breakdown." Kim started to cry again. "Look, Kim, I don't mean to sound cold, but I'm not for all this drama. Just drop me off, please. It's clear that you need some personal space right now."

Simone's response to Kim's actions served to settle Kim down. "Look, Simone, let's not make rash decisions. You know how I feel about you. Let me work this thing out. I'll get a handle on things and get this under control real soon. It won't take long, alright, girl?"

"Listen, Kim, what we do on the side is cool, but I'm not trying to do it exclusively. I don't see myself like that. You're starting to spook me out. I mean, what's next? You're gonna get a divorce? What then, we supposed to come out of the closet? Start going to gay/lesbian marches? What, we supposed to get married then? You might be going a little too far, Kim. Like I said, I'm not down with all of that."

All of that was a hard pill for Kim to swallow. She realized that she needed to step back and evaluate her situation. She pulled up to Simone's house. "Thank you for a good night. I enjoyed the dinner and the show. The company was shaky with all the drama though. Pull yourself together, girlfriend." Kim cleared her head. "I hear you, Simone. I'll get it together. Let me come inside with you."

Before Kim could undo her seat belt, Simone stopped her. "No, Kim. Not tonight, luv. Go home to your husband." Simone was just gaming Kim. She knew that her marriage was shattered. She knew that she now possessed Kim. "See if the thrill is gone or not." Kim reluctantly drove home to a house that was no longer a home.

CHAPTER 18

"Man, P, this some good eatin' right here." Paul had BBQ'd a brisket and turkey legs. "Yeah, man, I've been ready for this all game. The Giants are gonna smash them cowgirls. Football Sundays is what it's all about, baby. Show up or blow up, kid. The defense is back doing what they do. The G-men been breakin' up boys for years. Ask Joe Theisman and them Redskins, ask Tony Homo too. The Giants be chastising and brutalizing."

Mark didn't reply. Paul noticed his rowdy dog wasn't his normal self. "What's up with you, homie?" Mark snapped out of his reverie. "Shit, P, thangs is weighing heavy on a brother's mind." Mark had kept his long term affair with Alexis under wraps. He normally confided in Paul, but he kept that issue to himself. "Man, P, like I said, dog, shit is heavy." Mark proceeded to lace Paul up about the affair. He told Paul about how Alexis held him down during his bid and how Kim didn't. He even confided that he suspected Kim of currently having an affair.

"What?" Paul squealed. "That's some mind-blowing shit. I had no idea it was going down like that. For one, I didn't know that your sneaky ass was having an affair. You ain't even tell your boy? I can't believe that. I mean, I remember when you met honey, I was with you, but I didn't know that y'all took it there. And for this long? You a wild boy, bro. Then two, I didn't know that Kim fell off like that on you. You never said nothing about that. I can't believe that she shitted on you. Kim? I can't believe that."

"Yeah, well, believe it. I never said nothing because that's some embarrassing shit. That's a blow to a man's pride." "I can dig that, but yo, it's evident that you feelin' shawty. What you gonna do about that?" Mark shook his head. "That's just it, P. I don't know what to do, man.

I mean, Alexis proved her worth to me. When I was at my worst, she was still there. When I couldn't do for myself, she was there."

"I feel you, Mark. That shit counts for a lot." "You damn right it counts for a lot. She's a rider, man. Alexis is thorough, man. Kim on the other hand, let me down, P. She fizzled out on me. I can't point the finger at her for cheating though. Shit, look what I'm doing. What's cold is I'm really feelin' shorty, but I gots to hold on for Essence's sake."

Paul glanced at the TV. "Yeah, boyyy!" The Giants had the Cowboys down 14 to 3. He turned back to Mark. "I don't know what to say, bro. Kim is like family to me, but you gots to do what you feel is real. One thing you said is on point though. My goddaughter deserves the best. So for her sake, I understand you trying to keep it together."

Mark nodded his head in agreement. Paul continued on. "Peep this piece though, Mark. If shit ain't peaceful in the home, then that can affect Essence more than you living outside of the house. You feel me? If the crib is in chaos, then that will mess her up. If you and Kim split, as long as y'all stay civil, then it will work out as far as Essence is concerned. Y'all have to do the right thing - whatever is right for the both of y'all."

Mark was touched by Paul's insight. "I feel you, bro. That's real, kid."

****

Mark was paranoid and he began to get desperate. He increased his badgering of Kim concerning her activities. Kim continued to deny having an affair, but she was unconvincing. Her reply to Mark was always, "Your conscience is probably getting the best of you because of all of your lies and deception. You know what they say, Mark. When one starts accusing the other, it's because the accuser is guilty."

Mark just shook his head. "You can say what you want, but I know something ain't right. It like you're not yourself anymore. Someone or something got possession of you. I'm trying to make this work, but you don't care one way or another. Have you been taking Essence into consideration?"

At that, Kim scrunched up her face and placed her hand on her hips. "Essence? Apparently you was the one not taking her into consideration. Were you thinking about her when doing what you were doing to go to prison? That's what I thought. So don't get self-righteous on me." Kim stormed out of the house, slamming the door behind her

****

Mark had been trying to keep his distance from Alexis. He was missing her something terribly though. Daily he fought himself tooth and nail not to show up at her doorstep. He justified those thoughts with Kim's actions. He reasoned that Kim was pushing him into the arms of another woman. He was struggling with himself on the regular not to give into his desires.

Kim had been spending a lot of time out of the house. Her common excuse was that she was working, or at the gym, or with the girls. Mark never believed Kim's excuses, but one day, an unsuspecting call from Stephanie confirmed his suspicions. Mark looked at the phone disbelievingly. "She ain't here, Steph. She told me she was going out with you."

Stephanie got quiet because she knew that she had gotten Kim busted. "Oh, well maybe she's on her way here. Traffic probably heavy." Stephanie tried to cover for Kim. "Oh hell no! If she was coming to meet you, she would've been there. She left two hours ago. Listen, Stephanie, we need to talk. I need some answers." Stephanie hesitated. She didn't want any part of their drama. She felt that she had her own problems. "Listen, Mark, I don't know what's going on. I don't want to be thrown in the mix. Hell, both of y'all are like family to me."

Mark sucked his teeth. "Puh-leeze, Steph, was we like family when you showed up at the door trying to get your groove on?" The gloves were now off. Mark was desperate and willing to use any means to get set answers. "Oh hell no you didn't, Mark! You didn't have to take it there. That's cold-blooded. That was one drunken indiscretion."

Mark sucked his teeth again. "Damn all that, Steph. Get over here right now. I would come to you, but Essence is sleep." Stephanie herself had wondered what in the world was wrong with Kim. Kim wasn't her normal self anymore. Stephanie had no idea that Kim was using her to get out of the house. *Damn*, Stephanie thought. *She should have at least been on top of her game to let me know. She trying to be all sneaky and shit. Now look what happened. She's cold busted.*

Stephanie showed up to Mark and Kim's house soon after the phone call. "Listen," she said. "I told you I don't know what's going on." Mark slammed the door. "Stop fronting, Steph. You know something. You and Kim are best friends, right?" Stephanie smirked. "That's hard to tell. Truth be told, I'm just as concerned as you are." They both sat down and Mark attempted to get answers out of Stephanie. Mark quickly realized that Stephanie was just as in the dark as he was. He was reassured that Kim withheld her activities from Stephanie because she knew that Steph would tell Mark. Mark was right.

Kim often caught Stephanie watching Mark, but she never addressed it. She knew that her friend was attracted to her husband. At the time she trusted Mark and felt that he wouldn't betray her. Kim accepted Stephanie how she was. She wasn't blind though. She knew if Mark gave her the chance, she would quickly jump in the sack with him. She chose not to give Stephanie any ammunition against her. Therefore, she didn't tell Steph anything.

"Alright, Steph, thanks for coming over anyway. I'm just concerned about Kim. I'm in limbo here, and on the strength of Essence, I'm trying to fix it". Stephanie smiled. She tried hard, but she couldn't help herself. "Well, however this plays out between y'all, I'm still here, Mark. Whenever and however you need me, just call." She then hugged Mark and held the embrace a little too long. "I'm serious, Mark: whenever and however."

Mark's mind was consumed so he missed Stephanie's underlying sexual innuendos. He began searching the house. He moved methodically but felt possessed like a madman. After not finding anything of relevance, he ventured into Kim's walk-in closet. Mark rarely went into Kim's closet. He afforded her her personal space. He spotted Kim's trunk. He noticed that Kim had a padlock on the trunk. "What in the hell? What she got a lock on here for?" he wondered out loud.

Mark went to get a hammer. He was now on a mission and that personal space mumbo-jumbo was out the window. He was determined to get in the trunk. He was expecting to find pictures or letters from Kim's new man. He finally located the hammer and went to work on the trunk. It only took a few hacks to bust the lock open.

"Damnnnn," Mark sang. He rifled through the trunk and the contents were mind blowing. He began to question his own ability in the bedroom. "When did Kim get into all of this shit?" he wondered out loud. Inside the trunk were all of the sex toys that Simone had given Kim. Kim kept the toys and on occasion used them on herself.

"Kim changing like a muthafucker. I know that someone is introducing her to shit now. That girl ain't know about this type of shit. I know for a fact that she's cheating now." Mark took out all of Kim's toys and carried them into the living room. He carefully placed them on the coffee table. Mark lined them up like a prosecutor lines up damning exhibits or evidence.

****

Kim was still wrapped up in Simone's embrace. It was 2 in the morning. Kim dozed off in erotic bliss. Simone knew Kim's situation. She knew that she should've woken Kim up, but Kim looked so content. She gently stroked Kim's hair as Kim snored lightly and fell into a deeper sleep. Simone basked in the afterglow of their steamy rendezvous.

After a while Kim awoke with a start. She loosened herself from Simone's embrace to look at the clock. "OH MY GOD!" Kim exclaimed. "Mark is going to kill me! It's 2:45 in the morning!" Kim had never stayed out this late since Mark's return home. She expected Mark to explode.

Kim quickly showered and gathered her things. "I don't see why you just don't stay," Simone said. "What's done is done." Kim momentarily contemplated Simone's offer. "No, girl, I have to go. I wish I could stay. I want to stay, but its best I leave." Simone feigned an attitude. "So it's like that? I'm only good for a hit and run, huh? You talk about I'm playing games, but who's really playing games?"

Kim usually could be persuaded by Simone, but on this night, she knew that she had overdone it. She chose not to feed into Simone's bullshit and get home instead. She didn't know what to expect when she got home. She didn't want to make matters any worse.

****

Mark dozed off several times while waiting for Kim. Each time he looked at the toys on the table, it gave him a new source of energy. "This chick got a lot of nerve." The last time he glanced at the clock it was 2 o'clock. He dozed off again.

Kim opted not to park in the garage because she didn't want to make a lot of noise. She wanted to creep into the house undetected. She hoped like hell that Mark was asleep and that he wouldn't notice the time. Her hopes were crushed as soon as she opened the door.

When Kim turned around from locking the door she spotted her small cache of naughtiness. She froze at first with the nervousness of being busted, but that quickly gave way to anger. At the same time Mark came out of the bathroom.

He rushed to Kim and pushed her against the wall. It caught Kim of guard. In all their time together, Mark had never displayed violence towards her. "Mark, stop! Don't!" she screamed. "Where in the hell were you, Kim? It's 3 o'clock in the damn morning. You don't have no respect for me? No respect for our marriage? And what the hell is all of this?" He pointed to Kim's sex toys.

At that point Kim's anger had risen to the top. "That's a good damn question, Mark. What are you doing breakin' into my personal shit?" Mark pointed his finger in Kim's face. She scooted back to a newfound fear. "Don't you dare try to turn this shit around! If you weren't acting so damn suspicious and out of the ordinary, then I wouldn't have to search for shit. Now where were you?" Mark yelled.

Kim stammered. "I-I was out with the girls." "Who?" Mark questioned. Kim regained some of her gas. She sucked her teeth. "I was with Stephanie. Who else?" With that lie, Mark drew back his hand to slap Kim. "Nooo, Daddy, no!" Essence screamed.

All of the yelling had forced Essence out of her sleep. Essence's scream had snapped Mark out of his anger-induced state. He quickly rushed to her and picked her up. He kissed the tears out of her eyes as he carried her back to her room. "I'm so sorry, baby, I'm so sorry."

Essence continued to cry. "Why are you and Mommy fighting?" Mark had to compose himself, because seeing his baby hurt was tearing him apart. "It's just a misunderstanding, honey. Don't worry; everything will be okay."

Kim stood in the doorway of Essence's room and watched them. Mark stared in Kim's eyes. "Everything will be okay," he repeated. "Baby, go to sleep." He lay with Essence 'til she fell asleep. As he lay there, he couldn't believe it. He was getting ready to hit his wife. He had always frowned on abusive men and he was a split second away from being an abusive man himself. What was his life coming to? He dozed off to sleep with his pride and joy.

CHAPTER 19

That potentially violent episode with Mark managed to bring Kim back to reality. Seeing her little girl hurt and in tears was the motivation that she needed in order to regain control of herself. Kim had lost control of her natural self and come under control of the Sodom and Gomorrah side of herself. The spirit of perversion engulfed her, but she now had a renewed desire to break free of it.

"It's over, Simone. I can't do this anymore." Kim was crying uncontrollably. "This shit is starting to affect my baby now. Essence is starting to see the aftermath of my decisions."

"Aftermath of your decisions?" Simone was sick and tired of Kim. "It's like a seesaw messing with you, Kim. One minute it's on, then the next minute it's off. What's the deal with that? You had me go against my better judgment and fall for you. Now you trying to pull out? I don't understand this shit. So what now? What am I supposed to do?"

Kim blew her nose and composed herself. "Look, Simone, I don't know what to tell you. What can I say? This is definitely not what I wanted or intended. The fact of the matter is that it's all about Essence. She knows shit's not right with me and her father. Maybe Mark is right. We owe it to Essence to try harder. She deserves at least that much. I have to give it 100%. If it don't work, then fine. At least I would've tried."

Simone sucked her teeth and rolled her neck. "That's a load of bullshit. You know what I think?" Kim looked at Simone questioningly. "I think that you're just afraid to let go. I think that you're using poor little Essence as a crutch. I think that you're a coward, and that it's just easier for you to go with the norm, the traditional, the husband, the kids, the picket fence. I think you're scared to face who you really are."

It was Kim's turn to suck her teeth and roll her neck. "That's total bullshit, Simone. What you're talking about is neither here nor there. Like I said, it ain't about me, Mark, or you, for that matter. It's all about Essence, point blank, end of story. So what I said still stands. I must try harder. I have to forsake what I really want, which is you. I have to, as a mother, put Essence's interests first."

Simone thought to herself, *How am I to argue with that?* She knew that if she pushed too hard it was possible to push Kim away. Besides, she didn't want to appear like an insensitive ass. "Alright, alright, boo. I understand. I really do. You just promise me you won't forget about me. Promise me that you won't leave me hanging. Oh yeah, and promise me that if it don't work out with him, you'll come running back to my arms."

Kim began to cry again. She managed to get out, "I promise, I promise, I promise" in between sobs. Simone kissed her long and hard and passionately. "Make love to me like it's the last time." Kim's mouth formed to say no, but her tingling body screamed yes. Simone wanted to leave a lasting impression on Kim, an impression that would ultimately cause Kim to leave her husband.

CHAPTER 20

Mark and Kim's relationship slowly began rebounding. They tentatively began communicating again. They were both dedicated to repairing their marriage. The love that they had for Essence prompted them to salvage their union. Kim, however, was still a ball of confusion. She was still wrestling with her sexuality. Simone had completely blindsided her and unleashed desires that she didn't know existed within herself. That was her dilemma.

Kim began to evaluate her past to view if she suppressed these feelings throughout her life. She could not remember a time when she was ever attracted to women. This, she deduced, was all new. She had never looked at women in that light, but now she was consumed with the thought of love. She had a bad case of Simone-itis.

Mark was trying to be committed to his marriage. He truly wanted to revitalize his relationship. Like Kim, he was also a ball of confusion. Similar to a magnet, he found himself drawn to Alexis. The more he reflected about the way she held him down, the more he was magnetized. Their sex was explosive, the communication flowed easily, and Alexis had proven to be dependable. What more could you want in a woman? The more he thought about it, the more he developed a sense of obligation to Alexis.

Although he and Kim were back to communicating, they were currently sexually inactive. Not only was Kim wrestling with her newfound dilemma, she inwardly knew that Mark had cheated on her prior to going to prison. She used this as her chief excuse to not be intimate with Mark. She claimed that her lack of trust for him had dissolved her sexual attraction towards him. Mark did not push the issue. The truth of the matter was that he really didn't feel sexually inclined towards Kim either. He was trying to reconnect with her, but he was having a hard time doing so. Kim wasn't the same woman that he had married. She had undergone several changes - changes that Mark wasn't feeling. On some Forrest Gump shit, change was like a box of chocolates. You never know what you're gonna get. Change is definite, but what type of change - change for the best, or change for the worst?

Mark felt as though he didn't know this new Kim. Kim claimed that Serenity was the springboard that propelled her to evolve. She said that it was at Serenity where she vowed to never break or be weak again. The breakdown almost crushed Kim. She blamed that on her sheltered life and naiveté.

Kim's outlook on life hardened and this served as a defense mechanism. This hardness as a thought process was applied to everything, including her husband. It was as if Kim was imbued with Novocain. She was numb and void of feelings.

CHAPTER 21

"Combination shot, six ball in the corner pocket." Paul and Mark were hanging out at the local pool hall. "Yeah, boy! Some things don't ever change. You still can't touch me. I'm a beast at this." Paul cleared the table. The only thing left to do was sink the eight ball. The shot was a simple straightaway shot. Before Paul could make the shot, Mark took his stick and knocked the remaining balls from the table. "Uhhh damn, kid, you pressed like that?" They both laughed long and hard.

This was Mark's first time laughing all evening. They grabbed a few beers from the bar. "You been real quiet tonight, Mark. What's the deal, bro?" Mark just chuckled. He thought to himself, *Paul been knowing me for too long. He knows when shit ain't right wit' his boy. Ain't no sense in lying to him.* "You know, P, same ole same shit. Still on thin ice with wifey."

Paul wasn't surprised. He knew that something heavy was going down with his roadie. He just didn't know what. "I thought y'all was gonna work that out, homie." "Yeah, we was trying, dog. Shit is complicated right now though, P. It's like Kim turned into the ice queen and shit. She won't let a brother get close to her or nothing, if you know what I mean".

Paul thought about it. After a few seconds a "you gotta be kidding" look over came Paul's face. "You mean to tell me that once again you pussyless? No pu-pu, no parmagina, no va-jay-jay, no - "Before Paul could finish his tirade, Mark interrupted. "Chill, P, this shit is serious, man.""I am serious…shit!" Mark frowned and slammed his beer down.

"A'ight, a'ight. What's really going down, baby bro?" Mark sighed deeply. "Her excuse is that she thinks that I've slept with somebody else." Paul had a confused look on his face. "I thought y'all decided to move on and get over that. Is she changing her mind about that now?" Mark held a sheepish look on his face. "What?" Paul asked. "Let me find out that you didn't come all the way clean with Kim." Paul looked Mark in the face, saw the same sheepish look, and burst out laughing.

"Chill, chill, P. You don't understand, bro. Some things are hard to change. You know the code, man." Paul tried to regain some semblance of seriousness. "What code you talkin' 'bout, Mark?" "You know," Mark replied. "Deny 'til you die." Once again Paul burst out laughing. Mark began to get petulant. "Man up, P, this ain't no fuckin' comedy jam."

"Alright, Mark, damn. I don't understand though, man. Why you ain't just lay all the cards on the table? You know damn well Kim ain't no fool, bro." "She damn sure ain't," Mark agreed. "She figures that I've been cheating, so she's not trying to get intimate with a brother. That's one of her reasons, but I think it's just an excuse to be distant." Mark's pride wouldn't allow him to tell Paul about the sex toys that he'd found. "I think some shit might be going on."

Paul was at a loss of words. "This shit don't add up. If you didn't tell her you was cheating, then what is she basing shit on?" "Good question. She said since I was hiding hustling from her, then I could hide anything. She said she knows loose women come with the life of a hustler."

Paul nodded his head. "Well, she's right about that. Told you she's far from a fool." The two men got quiet as they delved into their thoughts. "Hold up. Hold up." "What?" Mark asked, startled by Paul. "You mean to tell me that you still getting it with shorty?"

Mark forcefully shook his head. "Naw, I stalled that out, man". Paul looked relieved. He really looked at Kim like a sister and he wanted their marriage to succeed. "Alright, Mark, just play your part and she'll come back around. Human nature is a beast, bro. She'll get right. Just stay down." Mark wanted to believe his boy, but he had his doubts. "Yeah, I hear you, P. It just might be a matter of time, like you said."

****

"I miss you, Kim," Simone cooed into the phone. Simone had resumed her pursuit of Kim. Kim wasn't trying to focus on her marriage, but her weakness for Simone was overbearing. "Come on now," Kim pleaded. "I thought that we agreed - "

"Yeah, yeah, I know. But we can still be cool, right? It ain't got to be all about the sex. I mean, I just miss your company. I miss having you around. I'd like to think that we had more than just the physical act of sex between us. Let's go out to a comedy club or something. Let's go to a concert, a movie, hell, even bingo. Let's do something…anything!"

Kim contemplated her answer. "Alright, Simone, I'll tell you what. We can roll, but Steph gotta roll too." Simone sucked her teeth. "Who is it that you don't trust? You either don't trust me, or you don't trust yourself." "Whatever," Kim replied. "Alright, if that's the way it gotta be, cool. Let's do this."

Kim felt that with Stephanie running interference, the chances of her and Simone crossing boundaries were lessened. Stephanie was in the blind; therefore it forced her and Simone to act accordingly. Simone's statement was dead on. She didn't trust Simone or herself to act right if they were alone. "Alright, girl, let's do this," Kim replied. "We can link up this weekend."

****

"I ain't heard from you in two months. All of a sudden you callin' me up outta the blue? What's up with that?" Jack, as a favor to Simone, got in touch with Stephanie. He had already grown tired of Stephanie and had written her off. Simone was determined to get one on one time with Kim by any means. This included getting Jack to hook up with Stephanie. "Come on, Steph, you know how shit be, boo. You know this crazy life I live, girl. I had to lay low out of town for a while."

Stephanie knew that Jack was a bad boy and that his story was possible. Also he was the bomb in bed and she needed, and wanted, to believe him. "I understand all that, Jack, but you could've at least called me. That ain't right."

"You right, but I'm callin' you now, right? So what's up? Can I see you or what?" Stephanie teased, "What you wanna see me for? I thought that you forgot about me. Come on, ma, how am I gonna forget about you? You just as nasty as me. I can't forget about you, Steph. You got that good-good."

Stephanie chuckled. "It's hard to tell. I ain't heard from you in two months." Jack wasn't on the phone to discuss or play games. "Look, we discussed that already. Now is you wit' it or not?" Stephanie quickly changed her song and dance. "Yeah, we can get together, but I was supposed to kick it with the girls tonight."

Jack got cocky. "Can the girls do you like I do you?" That was the push Stephanie needed to make up her mind. "Hell naw. Can't nobody do me like you," she said. "Come and pick me up and next time, don't take so long to get in touch with me."

CHAPTER 22

The night Jack chose to mysteriously reconnect with Stephanie was the night that Kim and Simone rekindled their flame. Kim tried to abstain, but Simone's pursuit was relentless. It was like the connection was never broken. The passion resumed and picked up right where it had left off. Once again, Kim was caught up in a whirlwind of complexity.

Soon after, bombs began to drop on Mark. "Kim, where in the hell you goin' now?" Mark yelled. "Out," Kim growled. "And don't question me like I'm a child. I'm grown." She walked out the door, slamming it. Their relationship was deteriorating quickly. Kim had lost and forsaken all of her wifely duties. She gave in to her innermost desires.

Kim's loss of control caused her to neglect her household. Mark was pissed off to the highest of pisstivity. "Kim got me messed up," Mark said. "Two can play this game." Once again, Mark's loneliness drove him to gravitate towards Alexis. Loneliness was the same engine that propelled him when Kim was in Serenity.

"Well, well, well. I thought you forgot about a sista." Mark chuckled. "That's the problem, Lex. I can't forget about you. Trust me, I've tried. Like the old saying goes, I can't get you out of my system." "So what are you trying to say Mark? You tryna see me now?"

Mark was at a crossroads once again. He was neglected, lonely, and his needs (both emotional and physical) were unmet. The only thing keeping him from running across the border was Essence. He was hanging on by the thinnest of threads. "I just wanted to see how you was doing, boo. Feel your vibe."

Alexis sensed Mark's hesitation and indecisiveness. She knew that Mark wanted her. She could feel his energy. Alexis could hear it in his voice. Even though Alexis wanted Mark beyond comprehension, she still had her pride. She was willing to play games to get to him, but she still had standards. Alexis didn't want Mark to come back to her in a moment of weakness. She wanted him to come back because his mind was made up. She didn't want temporary love; she wanted permanent love. She wanted a 'til death do us part kind of love.

"Yeah, I hear you, Mark. I'm doing okay. How are you doing?" They spoke civilly on the phone. They both laughed, reminisced, and they expressed how much they missed one another. "So how are things between you and the missus?" Alexis asked. Mark sighed. "Shit rockier than mountains. On the real, my marriage is in shambles."

Alexis sucked her teeth. "Oh, so you call me up, huh?" Mark imagined Alexis rolling her neck and turning up her lips. He had to laugh. "Busted. You got me, Lex." "I'm not trippin though. I mean, I hate to hear that you're hurting, boo-boo, but I can't front. I can't say that I'm sorry. I gots to be real here. I'm pleased to hear that your marriage is one step closer to being over. I know in my heart that when you're over that episode, you'll come back to me. All I have to do is sit back and let nature take its course."

Mark had to chuckle at Alexis's audacity. He was somewhat turned on by her boldness and confidence. She was sure and swift in her analysis. The reality of the situation was that she was dead on point. "You sound real sure of yourself, girl." It was Alexis's turn to chuckle. "Oh, I'm sure, alright. You said it yourself. You can't get me outta your system."

****

Kim began receiving late night calls on her cell phone. She guarded her phone as if her life depended on it. Mark began to notice this and he spoke on it. "I don't know what you're talkin' about Mark. You're acting so insecure lately. You know good and damn well I'm on call at the hospital." This gave Mark pause. He hadn't thought about that. "Yeah, I know that you're on call. I thought that's what the pager was for."

"Pager? That's so 80's. Welcome to the new millennium." Mark thought about it some more. Maybe he was being a tad bit insecure, but he had probable cause. "Yeah, whatever. If it was the hospital calling you, then why you be creeping out and talking all hush-hush for?"

Kim sighed as if she were being pestered. "It's called respect, Mark. I'm trying not to wake you up." Mark knew that Kim was lying. He could feel the coldness of Kim's lies in his entire being. He reflected once again on how much Kim had changed. She'd morphed into a sneaky, conniving, cheating liar. He had to chuckle because in all honesty, he wasn't far behind her.

****

"This some real live bullshit right here." Mark was furious. When he came out of the house to go to work, he found his car had been vandalized. As he stepped back into the house, the phone rang. "What?" Mark yelled into the phone. "Can I speak to Kim please?" a male voice asked.

"Who the fuck is this?" Mark questioned. Before he could get an answer, the unidentified caller hung up. Mark looked at the phone. "What the hell?" Mark was flabbergasted. Not only was his car vandalized, his wife was receiving calls from a strange man. He put the two together and deduced that Kim's lover had vandalized his car, then called knowing that she wasn't there. This was his way of telling Mark what was up.

****

"Thanks," Simone said. "That ought to spark something." Simone gave the teenager with the baritone voice a crispy Andrew Jackson for making the call. "No problem. Shit, that was the easiest change I ever made. You got any more calls that you need made?" he asked semi-jokingly. Simone had to chuckle herself. "Naw, homeboy. It's all good."

****

Mark was breathing fire. He was rendered incapable of sound reasoning. "Sir, Dr. Stevens is in with a patient right now." Mark disregarded this and brushed passed the receptionist. He forced himself into Kim's office. The receptionist quickly paged security. Kim was in the middle of a therapy session.

Hearing the door being pushed open forcefully alarmed Kim. Her patient was petrified upon seeing Mark's contorted face. He was frowning, breathing hard, and visibly shaking with rage. The patient wasn't the only one who was petrified. Kim was as well. She choked back her fear and made way for anger.

"What the hell are you doing, Mark? Why are you busting all up in my workplace?" Kim turned to her patient. "I'm so sorry, Ms. Kelly. This man is my husband, and apparently he's lost his damn mind." Before Mark could respond, he was gang tackled from behind by hospital security. He went down hard, but he came up swinging fast. When it was all said and done, Mark knocked out one officer and injured another. Mrs. Kelly, Kim's patient, fled the office. A brief second after Mark regained his sanity, he fled the office too. Kim was left in a state of bewilderment.

"Are you okay, Dr. Stevens?" the officer asked as he regained consciousness. "I'm fine, Amir. Are you going to be okay?" Not only had he gotten knocked out, but his pride was hurting. "I'm fine," replied Amir. "I know that man was your husband, therefore I won't press the issue. I do demand an apology from him though." Amir was supposed to report all infractions, but he liked Dr. Stevens. He appreciated her bedside manner. He'd witnessed so many rude doctors and

Dr. Stevens's care was refreshing. Her professionalism was the only thing that gave Amir pause in reporting the incident.

"I most definitely appreciate this, Amir. I certainly won't forget this. I will get to the bottom of this. You can rest assured that I will find out what's going on. I do apologize for all of this. Once again, I will get to the bottom of it. I will direct my husband to apologize to you directly. I'm sorry, Amir."

Officer Amir Michaels was working himself through law school. He was an even-tempered, mild-mannered guy. He was an optimistic eager-eyed fellow who thought that he could change the world. He was one of the few who believed in the justice system, and it had always been his dream to practice it.

He knew that Dr. Stevens's husband's rage wasn't directed towards him, the patients, or the hospital. *I don't know what's going on,* he thought, *but whatever it is, I bet Dr. Stevens is to blame. That man was mad as hell. His behavior is indicative of one who seeks answers.*

****

Kim was rattled for the remainder of the day. She could barely function. She floated throughout the rest of the day in a fog. She'd never seen Mark behave like that before. Kim didn't know exactly why Mark had come to her job in such a manner, but she suspected why.

****

"What's going on with you, Mark? I hope that everything is alright, boo-boo." After acting a fool at the hospital, Mark drove around aimlessly. He struggled to regain control of himself. After hours pf drifting, he arrived at Alexis's boutique. It was like the car's GPS system sensed its master's distress and automatically engaged the auto pilot button. When Mark refocused, he realized that he was parked in front of Alexis's boutique.

"I need you, Alexis." That's all Alexis needed to hear. She immediately took action. "I got you, boo. Come with mama." Mark blindly followed Alexis as she led him out of the boutique. He was willing to follow her anywhere at this point. While en route, Alexis booked a suite at the W hotel. Her intentions were to pamper Mark and give him what he needed - whatever that was.

She wasn't aware of what had happened yet, but she knew that whatever it was, it was serious. Mark was in a zombie-like state. They remained quiet during the whole drive. Within this quietness, they were connecting on a whole 'nother plane.

Once they entered the suite, Mark collapsed into Alexis's arms. She quickly undressed him and led him to the bathroom's large oval-shaped Jacuzzi. Alexis filled the tub with hot water and bubbles and then turned the jets on.

Mark immersed himself in the soothing aura of the tub. He closed his eyes and allowed Alexis's fingers to work their magic. After a few blissful minutes, he felt the anxiety ebb out of his being. Alexis could feel the tension slackening in Mark's muscles. Mark was in a state of vulnerability. Alexis realized that he was fragile. She felt that Mark was on the brink of something; she just wasn't sure what.

Alexis chose to let Mark broach the subject of his current state. She didn't want to rush him or allow her satisfaction to betray her. She surmised that his current state involved his wife. She didn't want Mark to know that his misery, at the moment, was her satisfaction.

After about an hour Mark was content and removed from the previous drama of the day. Kim tried to contact Mark during his de-stressing session, but after several attempts, she gave up. Mark turned his cell phone off and turned himself over to the instant gratification that Alexis provided. The magic that Alexis worked was equivalent to the pinnacle of pure ecstasy.

****

"I can't believe Mark," Kim complained to Stephanie. "That Negro had the nerve to come to my job and bust all up in my office - not to mention I had a patient at the time, mind you. He ended up jumping on the security officer and everything. He was like a possessed madman, girl. I could've sworn he wanted to jump on me too, Steph."

Stephanie was shocked. She never imagined Mark flipping out on Kim like that. "Why is he trippin', Kim? There's got to be a reason." Kim simply shrugged her shoulders. "Hell if I know."

****

Mark drifted off into a deep, peaceful sleep. His last thoughts were of how things were opposite as far as Kim and Alexis were concerned. As of late, Kim represented chaos and drama. Alexis, on the other hand, represented peace and calmness. He lay on Alexis's bosom like a suckling babe with the blanket that only peace could bring.

On that particular night, Mark's mind was made up for him. He chose to discontinue his marriage and embark on a new journey with Alexis. Mark vowed to continue to be the best father he could be to Essence. He realized that he couldn't be the best father while still being with Kim and the attached drama. He woke up from the best sleep that he had in a long while. "Lex, wake up."

Alexis woke up with a start. "What's wrong, boo?" She looked up into Mark's smiling face."Ain't nothing wrong, girl. Everything is all to the right. We are right together, baby." Alexis knew what was coming and she braced herself for it. She'd been ready for this day since meeting Mark. "Baby, I never made a promise that I didn't intend to keep. I told you from jump that if things didn't work out with me and Kim, then it would be me and you." Alexis's eyes lit up like the Fourth of July. "If you'll still have me, Lex, you got me. I plan on divorcing Kim and being with you."

Inside, Alexis was doing backflips and somersaults. Outside, she displayed a quiet coolness. "Are you sure that's what you want, boo? I don't want you to do anything that you'll live to regret." Mark smiled. "Yeah, I'm sure, Lex. Shit, you've proven to be the woman that I need on every level. I have no doubts. You've held me down when I needed it and lifted me up when I needed that too. Straight up, it's all about you now, boo."

CHAPTER 23

  Kim was beside herself. She experienced every level of full rage emotions. She knew that her marriage was over, but she was still surprised that Mark had actually left her. She was appalled at finding out what had sent Mark into a frenzy. Mark claimed that his car had been vandalized and that he had received a call from a man afterwards asking for her.

  Kim didn't believe Mark. Inwardly, she felt Mark had created an excuse in order to leave her. Kim ran her theory by Simone. Simone agreed with Kim. "He's just a coward. Instead of manning up and calling it quits, it sounds like he created an excuse. That's just like a man too. They always seem too look for the easy way out. Such a freakin' coward."

****

  Kim had come home from a long shift to find Mark gone. She didn't realize it initially until she looked inside his walk-in closet. All of his belongings were missing. Mark's closet looked as if it belonged in a vacant house. Kim sat down in Mark's closet and cried. She wasn't crying for the loss of Mark so much, but the failure that she incurred. She was relieved that Mark left, but at the same time saddened.

  Kim realized that she'd lost control of herself a while ago. She knew that Mark was a good man. She knew that she was blessed to have him as a father to her child. Like a thief in the night, she allowed doubt and lust to come in and crumble the foundation of their union. Kim accepted this fact and she was set to move forward with Simone.

****

"Oh, so I'm the consolation prize, huh? What? I guess I'm supposed to be all happy-go-lucky now, right?" Kim was taken aback. She expected Simone to be happy that they could finally be together exclusively.

"I feel like a damn runner-up or something. It's not like you left him to be with me, right? The fact of the matter is that he left you. So now you wanna come running to me, and what? I'm supposed to be ecstatic? I'm not sure how I feel about that, Kim. I know that I'm not feeling that at all." Kim began to have a panic attack. She felt as if her world was crushing her.

****

Mark was settling in nicely at Alexis's place. As opposed to his former residence with Kim, this one was like an oasis in paradise. He somewhat expected Kim to roadblock his visiting with Essence, but it was just the opposite. Kim seemed to be regressing to the state that she was in before going to Serenity. Mark wasn't ready to expose Essence to other women. He wanted to make sure that he and Alexis would be able to stand the test of time before introducing the two.

****

Kim was enraged that Simone had been neglecting her. She'd tried to connect with Simone, but her attempts proved to be futile. The times that Kim was able to corner Simone, Simone managed to wiggle out of her grasp. Kim's calls went unanswered, as did the knocks on the door. Kim worked herself up to a boiling point. She began thinking irrationally.

Waking out of a fog, Kim found herself parked outside of Simone's apartment. Her breathing had turned frantic over the course of the time and she was struggling to regain control. In her frenzied, rage-filled zone, she forgot to breathe. Her sympathetic system was working overtime. She attempted to separate from her emotions and focus, but the task at that point in time was the unmanageable.

"This bitch is playing games with the wrong chick. I've sacrificed everything for her. Now she pulls this shit? I am not the one. I refuse to play the weakling ever again in life." Kim sat outside Simone's house for nearly two hours. She was expecting to catch Simone cheating, but hoping that that wasn't the case. There was no other excuse for Simone's actions. After two hours, there was no traffic to or from Simone's apartment. Kim's irrational and illogical mind frame began to work harder.

****

"Damn, boo, that feels so good." Mark had wanted to spoil Alexis rotten. She'd brought him so much peace as of late that he felt like she deserved it. "Don't stop what you're doing, bae." When Alexis had walked through the door, she had been greeted with pampering, catering, and complete service.

Mark spent the day cooking, cleaning, and pampering her. The menu consisted of Cornish hens, wild rice, broccoli with cheese, and French bread. For dessert he ordered her favorite cheesecake from Junior's. After making sure the house was spotless, Mark trooped over to the barbershop. He wanted to look his best for Alexis. Before returning home, he stopped by Bath and Body. He decided to pick up some aromatherapy bath products, candles, and lotions.

"I won't stop, baby, 'til' you tell me to." In the background, Maxwell's "Til the Cops Come Knockin' " was playing. Mark engaged in massaging Alexis from head to toe. When he finally reached her feet, he inserted her toes one by one into his warm, inviting mouth. His aim was to please and he wouldn't stop 'til pleasure was achieved. Alexis was completely wrapped up in the rapture. She was floating on a cloud of feather-covered bliss. "Damn, baby, you're just too good to me."

****

Before Kim could restrain herself, she found herself inside Simone's apartment. Her crashing through the front window barely registered in her twisted brain. She expected to find Simone in the arms of another. Kim tried to contain herself and get her bearings straight. The only thing that she could hear was her heartbeat pounding in her ears.

****

Alexis jumped out of her sleep. Mark was moving fast now. "What is it, baby?" Alexis asked. "Nothing, baby, go back to sleep, I thought I heard something, that's all." Ever since Mark's car had been vandalized, he slept lightly. He rushed to the window and peered out at his automobile. To his relief, his car was as he'd left it. "I gots to get over this shit, man," he said, trudging back to bed.

****

Kim gave way to her emotions, and it was like a light switch had been flipped on. Kim methodically searched every room, not sure what she was looking for. She had visualized finding Simone in the ecstatic act of lovemaking. She was relieved at not finding her visualizations manifested. She was relieved due to the fact that she didn't trust herself if her suspicions were confirmed.

She was already acting in a manner in which she'd never acted before. She didn't know just how far she would, or could, go. After the wave of relief subsided, anger reemerged. Her rampant imagination retook control. She flashed back to her failed marriage, her now failed relationship with Simone, and her breakdown. Once again rage took control. She was angered by the curveballs life threw her way.

Kim began smashing all of the fragile items in the living room. The clown figurines that Simone treasured were smashed under her feet. The Tiffany lamps that Simone adored were shattered. The movie theater-style sectionals were slashed beyond repair. Kim received instant gratification as the rage slowly worked its way through her system. Kim was breathing so deeply and rapidly that she was lightheaded. Her chest heaved in and out as perspiration flowed freely down her face. It was like a faucet had been turned on due to her exertion.

"I'll kill this bitch!" Kim screamed. Her adrenaline was pumping overtime. She made her way into the bedroom and stripped the bed of its linen. She brought the sheets to her nose, expecting to find the remnants of a scent that revealed a torrid episode. "How dare she?" Kim screamed. She flung the sheets, tossed the comforter, and flipped the mattress over in a frenzied act of despair.

"What in the hell?" Kim paused. Under the mattress on the box spring, Kim spotted a red book. Upon closer look, she noticed that it was a diary. Kim quickly snatched it up. She clutched it as if it held all life's hidden answers. Something in Kim's mind clicked. She expertly re-made the bed. She didn't want to draw any attention to the bed since she'd found its hidden treasure.

Kim decided to take the TV and computer in order to make the break-in look like a bonafide burglary. She sped away from Simone's after the smash and grab. Her mind was racing 100 MPH. She couldn't get home fast enough. The anticipation of uncovering Simone's secrets drove Kim to the brink of being a nervous wreck. Little did Kim know that the pad only served as Simone's love nest. She actually resided elsewhere.

CHAPTER 24

Kim came to again at the sound of Simone's voice. She tried to bring herself upright, but it was hopeless. She was handcuffed to the headboard and her movement caused the cuffs to bite into her flesh. Her mind was cloudy. She had forgotten that Simone had hooked her up to the bed. Her words managed to break through the fog that the clouds brought.

"You can't seem to get the message, bitch. Why can't you just go away?" Simone was standing over Kim, shaking uncontrollably. Since you won't go away on your own, I'll make sure you go away permanently!" Kim knew that she was in trouble. The clouds quickly dissipated. If she didn't keep Simone talking, then she was a goner. "I don't understand what's going on, baby. I don't know what you're talking about. Why are you flippin' out like this? You got me so confused right now, Simone."

Simone was like a bull that had seen a red flag. She exploded. "Stop calling me that shit!" she yelled. "But I don't understand, baby. Stop calling you what?" Simone sucked her teeth. "I'm not your fuckin' baby and my name ain't Simone." Kim was taken aback. "What?"

Simone was ready to let the cat out of the bag. "My name is Alexis, bitch." Kim was stunned. "Alexis?" "That's right, Alexis. With you out of the picture, I'll have Mark all to myself." With that, Kim passed back out.

****

As Kim faded in and out of consciousness, she wondered, *How did I get to this point? What wrong turn in my life drove me to being handcuffed to this bed? What choices led me to being drugged by my lover, and now on the brink of death? What decisions pushed me to cheat on my husband Mark? Damn, I have to try and stay awake.* The darkness kept pulling her closer though. It seemed so peaceful in the dark. It felt like a place void of any drama. *I am so tired of drama. God knows my life has been drama-filled as of late. How did I get to this? How did I, Dr. Kimberly Stevens, a well-known psychologist, allow myself to go out like this? Oh no! Another wave of darkness.*

****

Kim managed to persuade Simone to meet her at her apartment. Simone was tired and completely through with Kim. Kim had transformed into a clingy, needy bug-a-boo. Simone's mission concerning Kim was drawn to a close. The purpose had already been served. Her relationship with Kim was designed to develop a wedge between Kim and Mark. The goal had been met.

Simone's – Alexis's - sole purpose was to get Mark by any means necessary. She saw that Mark straddled the fence and she determined that he needed help. This being the case, she decided to target Kim and turn her out. Alexis deduced that if she could make Kim leave Mark, then her desires could be met. While Mark was at his lowest and Kim at her most vulnerable, Alexis struck. With Kim out of the equation, Mark was now hers for the taking.

****

"Don't worry, I'll be a good mother to little Essence. You can rest in peace knowing that." Hearing that brought Kim back out of her fog. "What kind of sick-ass games are you playing, Simone?" She turned to Kim with a faraway, deranged look in her eyes. "Bitch, I done told you not to call me that. My name is Alexis. And best believe that this is not a game, sweetie."

Kim shook her head in an attempt to clear the cobwebs. "I just don't understand what's going on Sim- I mean, Alexis." A look of satisfaction overcame Alexis's face. "Alright then. Let me just tell you what's going on. When you went in the crazy house, I met Mark. I knew that I wanted him from the jump, but he thought that he loved you. I knew that it was just a matter of time before he woke up. All I had to do was play my position. He wanted me, but he just didn't know it. I helped open up his eyes though. Now that man is all mines."

"What are you talking about?" "I played my position. I was the woman that he needed at all times. When he was jobless and ass out, who did he turn to? That's right, sweetie, he turned to me. He didn't have no income so I hooked him up with my cousin Rondue. You may know him as Jack."

"Jack?" *Oh my God! You mean to tell me that this scary bitch even dragged Stephanie into this?* "That's right, bitch, Jack! I had to sic him on Stephanie's hot ass so I could get you alone. Anyway, when you came out of the loony bin, this nigga got to acting all confused. He got to talkin' 'bout 'we can't be together no more'. So I had to fix the situation to show him who would really ride with him to the end."

"What situation?" Kim asked, confused. "Fix it how?" Alexis sucked her teeth. "If your stupid ass would shut the fuck up, I'll tell you. In life I've learned that only time will reveal who's really down for you. I needed Mark to see this, so I had to get down for my crown." Kim looked at Alexis expectantly. "I tipped the police off to Mark's operations. I needed to show him that you'd fall off over time and I'd still be there."

This bitch is crazier than hell, Kim thought. "Sure as shit don't stink, that's what happened too. You failed Mark. When he was at his lowest, what did your sorry ass do?" Kim looked at her in disbelief. "Oh, now you can't talk? I'll tell you what you did then. You fell the fuck off. While you was off gallivanting around in a lesbo affair, I was there for Mark. We talked about everything. While I was being a friend to him, he told me about his suggestion to you about joining a gym. You were so easy. I can't believe you never swung that way. You practically threw yourself at me. Anyway, Mark came home and I thought he'd seen the light. He'd seen that you didn't really love him. Because if you did, then you wouldn't have fell off. When he came home, what did you do then?"

Kim still didn't answer Alexis. She lay in shock due to the whole ordeal. "I'll tell you what you did. You held innocent little Essence over his head. That's what you did, Kim. He recommitted to y'all's imaginary little relationship on the strength of Essence. Mark's a good man, and that's what good men do. It wasn't about you, Ms. Thang. It was all about the baby. So since Mark wasn't strong enough to leave you, I had to make you leave him.

Your hot ass couldn't wait to leave him either. You're a damn fool to run away from that good man. You tried to front at first, but the language that your body spoke told a whole 'nother story. "You talkin 'bout you never did this before. Shiiitttt! So-called best friend Stephanie probably been dagging for years."

Kim thought about their college years when they experimented. She sucked her teeth. Alexis continued to speak. "Anyway, when I gained the upper hand, I struck." Alexis and Kim locked eyes. "Mark isn't blind, you know. He knew that you were cheating. Since I'm his friend, we talked about things like that too. That's why when I vandalized his car. That was the straw that broke the camel's back. It was too obvious that your 'new man' did the deed."

"What? That was you?" Kim screamed. She went from being scared to mad. "Yes, that was me, sweetie." Alexis's eyes held a smile in them. Kim was too through. "I can't believe this shit. You are one sneaky, conniving, manipulating - " "Don't even say it. Because, sweetheart, what I really am is love-struck. I love Mark, and he loves me. In case you didn't know, we currently live together. In the blink of an eye, it'll just be Essence, Mark, and me. Like I said, I'll be a good mother to Essence." That faraway deranged look came back in Alexis's eyes.

"Listen, uh, Alexis, you don't have to do anything crazy. You can have Mark, girl. Truth of the matter is, you turned me out. I can't lie to myself anymore. I'm going to find me a new woman. If I'm lucky, I'll find someone a little like you. Maybe it's best if Essence stays with y'all. This way she won't be exposed to my new lifestyle."

Alexis let out a long, harsh laugh. "What I look like to you? I'm not gonna keep going through this back and forth shit with you. This ain't my first rodeo. I been through this shit before." Alexis regained that faraway look again as her mind traveled to some tumultuous years past.

****

"What do you mean we can't keep doing this? It's my birthday. I thought you loved me." Sam couldn't even bring himself to look at Alexis. He knew that he was dead wrong. Up until this point he had molested and manipulated a young Alexis for seven years.

It first began against Alexis's will. While Evelyn, Alexis's mother, was busy living the high life, she neglected Alexis. Over the course of time Alexis began to crave Sam's advances. Sam brainwashed Alexis to think that he genuinely loved her. In Alexis's immature, twisted mind, Sam was her man.

"I'm saying, Alexis, we can't do this anymore. If your mother even found out, she'd kill both of us." Alexis could not even fathom losing Sam. "She won't find out, baby. She hasn't found out thus far, right?" Sam's sick, pedophiliac brain wanted to give in. He was at a crossroads. At the moment he felt a twinge of guilt, but his true self would eventually take its toll.

"Naw, Lex, you deserve more than this. On the real, your moms deserves more than this."

Alexis attempted to use the only tool that she thought she possessed. "Okay then, at least be with me one last time. It's my birthday. You can at least do that for me? Let me give you something to remind you of me, baby."

Alexis knew Sam's weakness. Sam wrestled with himself like Job wrestled with God. His perverted spirit within beat him down like the po-po's beat down Rodney King. "Alright, Lex, but this gots to be the very last time."

Alexis performed every sick trick that Sam liked. He had begun grooming her to his pleasures at a young age. Her sole desire was to change his mind about the status of their relationship. She gathered that if she performed extraordinarily, then he would give into her wishes.

After the act was over, Sam was overwhelmed with guilt. He'd always felt a little guilty about molesting Alexis throughout the years, but he'd never experienced a feeling so great. Sam gathered his clothes with a heavy heart. In the back of his mind he wasn't sure if he had a newfound feeling of guilt, or if Alexis's coming of age was the issue. The pedophile in Sam was attracted to the young. To him, the younger the better. Whatever the case may have been, Alexis could sense Sam's withdrawal.

"So what now?" Alexis asked. Sam summoned his strength. It was as if he was on a cliff and the slightest bit of wind could blow him off the edge. He decided to speak before he gave into his sick nature. "I already told you, Lex. It's over! It stops now - not now, but right now. You have to go on with your life and I have to fix this with Evelyn."

All Alexis could think of was Sam's betrayal. She couldn't see him for the monster he really was. A creature such as Sam was a destroyer of one's future. He was a dream shatterer. Alexis was still a child who was blinded and brainwashed. In her sabotaged mind, she was in love. She vowed that if she couldn't have Sam, then no one could - not even her mother.

When Sam turned to walk out of her room, the scared little girl in her finally struck back. She swung with all of her might, hitting Sam in the head. After being depleted of her temporary courage, she stood in shock. She trembled as the hammer dropped at her feet. When Alexis realized she had killed the man of her life, she let out a piercing scream. She screamed for her innocence lost due to lies, deception, and the perception of love.

Alexis's mother Evelyn came running upon hearing her only child's wailing. What she stumbled upon was the nightmare that woke her up from her fairytale dream. Her free ride had prematurely come to an end. Like Alexis, she too wailed. Her wailing wasn't that of a concerned mother. Her wailing was one that signified the hard times to come.

Before the police could arrive, Evelyn decided to do the responsible thing. She decided to take claim of the situation. She never talked to Alexis about the truth. She chose to accept the implied truth. It was a lot easier for Evelyn to digest the fact that her daughter Alexis fought off a sexual attempt by hitting Sam with a ball peen hammer. Reality is what one perceives it to be. One person's reality maybe different from another's, based on perceptions.

****

Alexis snapped back to the present. "Like I said, bitch, I'm not gonna keep going through this shit. As long as you're around, you'll keep holding Essence over his head. You'll try to confuse him and take him from me. I can't have that, boo. I've invested too much in Mark to go out like that."

For the first time Kim was able to see Alexis for who she really was. She was a bruised, battered, and deranged young lady. Sam had contaminated Alexis at a young age. She viewed life through a twisted vision.

"Invested too much? I'm the one who invested too much. I've invested my whole life in Mark." Alexis smiled. "Yeah, you invested your whole life. Now you're getting ready to give your life too. Besides, you've already cashed in your investment for some pussy."

CHAPTER 25

In Alexis's trembling hands, she held a .38 Smith and Wesson lady model snub nose. "Well, Kim, I can't front. It was fun while it lasted, boo. Unlike you, I've never been with a woman before. I admit it wasn't that bad though." Alexis chuckled. "But like I said, ya gots to go. Your services are no longer needed." Alexis slowly raised the gun as nervous trails of perspiration tracked her face. Her hands shook with such force that she nearly dropped the gun. With forced determination, she added pressure to the trigger.

"Wait!" Kim yelled. "Can't no man be worth murder. Just think, Alexis. Can you go on happily ever after with your life knowing that you took mine from Mark?" A smirk slowly crossed Alexis's face. "True love is worth anything, honey child." It was now Kim's turn to smirk. "How can it be love if it was based on a lie?"

Frustrated, Alexis lowered her gun. "A lie? What lie? Mark loves me, and I love him. That's all there is to it – period, end of story." Sensing death around the corner gave Kim a false sense of bravado. Kim sucked her teeth, exasperated. With attitude, she asked, "What lie? You've gotta be kidding me! Girl, you lied your ass off to Mark from the jump. The whole sneaky way you misled him to the way you orchestrated his downfall was a lie. The way you seduced me to create easier access to him was a lie. Him getting robbed was a lie. How can he love you? The real you ain't shit but a lying, conniving bitch."

Now filled with rage, Alexis quickly raised the gun again. This time it didn't shake in trembling hands. This time she was focused and resolved to completing the task at hand. Kim felt the end closing in when their eyes locked. A lot of communication was transferred between the two women through more eye contact. Kim felt Alexis's hate, jealousy, and contempt. Alexis felt

Kim's pity, sorrow, and understanding. Feeling Kim's pity further fueled Alexis's anger. As Alexis applied pressure to the trigger, Kim closed her eyes.

****

Mark was flabbergasted. He could not believe what he was hearing. Never in a million years did he think that he would be caught up in a web of deceit. He was positioned outside of the bedroom where Alexis held Kim. He could hear the delirium laced not only in Alexis's words, but also in her voice.

Mark had received a crazy phone call from Kim. Kim claimed that she knew the truth about Alexis. After capturing Mark's attention, she proceeded to inform Mark of that truth. Kim warned that if he cared anything about her or Essence then he'd come. Knowing that Mark would show, she gave him the address to Alexis's hideaway. With Mark's assurance that he would come, Kim carried out her mission.

As Alexis walked through each step of her quest of Mark to Kim, things became clear to Mark. A lot of things began to add up. *Damn, this is one cold bitch*, Mark thought. He had often wondered about the coincidences of how things went down. Now things were crystal clear. *All this time I been sleeping with the enemy.*

Just when Mark was beginning to think Alexis was the one for him, the veil had been lifted from his eyes. Never in his life had he been exposed to such a calculated, cold-hearted deception. Never did he imagine that one woman could wreak so much havoc. The veil had been lifted and his feelings for Alexis changed in one fell swoop. As the old cliché goes, there's a thin line between love and hate.

Instead of accepting some of the blame, he shifted all of the blame onto Alexis. *It's all this bitch's fault why my marriage is destroyed*, he fumed inwardly. *It's all her fault why I got in the game, got robbed, and went to prison. She's a real live black widow. This crazy bitch even killed her step-pops, now she finna kill my wife.* Mark's love for Alexis quickly dissipated, turning to hate.

He continued to listen to Kim. Everything she said was exactly how Mark felt. Finally Mark had heard enough and decided to put an end to the bullshit. When he slid in the room, he was taken aback. He was shocked to see his wife handcuffed to the bed. He was even more shocked to see his mistress standing over her with a gun in her hands. His wife's eyes were closed tightly and she seemed to be praying.

Alexis was so locked in on Kim that she didn't even hear Mark enter the room. "You can say what you want, luv. Just know this before you go: I did what I had to do. Mark belongs to me now. He's all mine." Kim's eyes were still shut tight. She hadn't witnessed Mark's entry either. She was too busy praying and preparing for the inevitable.

"So you grimy like that huh, Lex?" Kim's eyes popped open upon hearing Mark's voice. Alexis spun around. "Mark?" Alexis gasped. "What are you - " "What, doing here?" Mark interrupted. "You surprised to see me? I'm glad that I'm here. It all makes sense now."

Alexis was frantic. "What are you talking about, baby?" Mark sucked his teeth. "Come off it, Lex, I done heard the whole play. I can't front; you got yours off. You one sick bitch." "But…but baby, I'm doing this for us."

"US? US! Bitch, you really done lost your mind, huh? I must look like Willy foo-foo or something to this chick," Mark wondered out loud. At that, Kim smirked. Alexis, upon seeing Kim's smirk, was propelled into a frenzy. "What'chu mean, Mark?" Alexis whined. "What are you trying to say? I know that you're not trying to say there's no us now. That's what you're saying?"

Mark chuckled. "What you think, Lex? You think I'm down with getting played? You think I'm down with seeing my wife, the mother of my child, handcuffed to a bed? You think spending time in jail was cool with me? Us? There is no us, Alexis. You old news, ma. I suggest you check yourself into a treatment center or something. You're in desperate need of help, Lex, for real."

Alexis levelled her gun at Kim. Kim shut her eyes again, bracing herself, expecting the blast to come. "Hold up, Lex!" Mark screamed, rushing closer. "What?" Alexis screamed, spinning around, aiming at Mark now. "You trying to save this bitch? For real? Let me guess: you think that y'all going to be together now? Shit, you think it's gonna be a happily ever after in all of this? Well, you got me fucked up if you think that." Alexis turned the gun back towards Kim. "If I can't have you, then I'll be damned if she can."

Mark charged between Alexis and Kim. At the same time, Alexis fired her gun. There were three screams ringing simultaneously. Kim's eyes remained closed until she heard a thud hit the floor. Her eyes met Alexis's after registering Mark's crumpled body on the floor. Once Alexis comprehended the magnitude of her actions, she again let out a piercing scream. She couldn't believe that she had just shot the love of her life. Alexis was now beside herself.

Alexis threw the gun down and rushed to Mark's lifeless form. "Mark!" she screamed. "Get up, baby!" She tried unsuccessfully to raise him up. "He's gone, Alexis. You've killed him," Kim stated. "He's the second man that you've killed because of your twisted take on love. First your stepfather; now Mark."

"Nooooo!" Alexis screamed. "You shut your fuckin' mouth, bitch!" Alexis crumpled down to Mark's spiritless side. "No, Mark, baby, please wake up!"

In the distance, a cacophony of sirens could be heard. Someone had called the police. In the solitude of the peace and quiet, the gun's report sounded like a cannon.

The siren's shrill song penetrated the fog of Alexis's psychotic mind. It caused her panic to elevate to the next level. She looked in Kim's accusing eyes. She felt convicted. "You just don't understand, Kim. Maybe you've never been in love like this before." Alexis looked down at Mark again. His life's existence pooled underneath him. The image of Mark unhinged her.

Without warning Alexis whirled around and scooped up the gun. "Oh shit!" Kim yelled. She knew that this was it. She could feel it. "Don't!" she screamed. "Don't do it!" She shut her eyes again, praying for a savior. For the second time the .38 came to life. For the second time, Kim's eyes remained closed 'til she heard a thud hit the floor.

Kim's eyes sprang open. "I'm alive," she whispered. Tears rushed from her eyes like water bursting through a damn. Lying across Mark's body was Alexis's. *Damn*, thought Kim. *This is the ultimate display of love. This was one sick bitch. Better her than me.* Kim let out a sick laugh.

CHAPTER 26

Upon hearing the shot, the police rammed in the front door. The grisly scene displayed before them answered all of their questions. The evidence was all self-explanatory. As far as the detectives were concerned, it was an open and shut case.

When they reached Kim, it was as if a movie director had yelled "action". Kim played the role of a lifetime, worthy of an Oscar. "Help me, help me!" she screamed. "Thank God you're here! Please get these cuffs off me!" In this scene, Dr. Kimberly Stevens played the role of a kidnapping victim. She cried, shook, and withdrew into herself as she hugged her knees. She rocked back and forth as she mumbled incoherently.

"Ma'am, are you hurt in any way?" the female officer asked. Before they questioned Kim, they chose to let an EMT team check her out. After clearing her, the officers were given the go ahead. "Ma'am, can you tell us what happened here?" Kim gave the appearance of trying to compose herself. "This is probably all my fault," she cried. "I should've handled this directly," she gushed.

"Calm down, ma'am," the female officer said. "Okay, okay." Kim sucked it up. "Well, I found out that my husband Mark was cheating with this woman. I chose to confront her about it. When I got here, she pulled a gun on me. She handcuffed me to the bed. I thought that she was going to kill me.

"Anyway, after a while my husband showed up. After seeing me, they began to argue. He told her that he won't leave me for her. She flipped out and shot Mark." Kim let out some tears for added effect. Officer Calhoun, the female officer taking the report, sensed that Kim was going to start up again. "You're doing good, Dr. Stevens. What happened then?" she asked in order to redirect Kim.

"After Mark fell to the ground I shut my eyes, thinking that I was next. I heard a shot, and when I opened my eyes, she was as you found her." This seemed to satisfy the detectives. "Okay, ma'am, if we need anything further, we'll get in touch. You are free to go. Do you need us to contact anyone to come get you?"

In Kim's mind she heard the director yell. "And...cut!" "No, I can make it from here," Kim answered. Officer Calhoun watched Kim curiously.

EPILOGUE

When Kim stumbled upon Alexis's diary, it pushed her over the edge. It was at this point when she began to devise her elaborate production. Up until then, she had fallen head over heels for Alexis. Until finding the diary, Kim was willing to go all the way with Alexis.

She'd battled her guilt and state of confusion. She was now content to overcome the stigmas attached and associated with her newfound lifestyle. Kim had unknowingly reduced herself to being a slave. She had become a slave to her lower self, a slave to sex, a slave to the almighty orgasm. The diary served as Kim's emancipation. It broke the spell of instant gratification.

"Damn, this bitch is good," Kim said while reading the diary. She couldn't believe all of Alexis's exploits in order to obtain Mark. The appearance of loyalty is a strong tool. The irony of the whole thing didn't escape Kim. She was willing to throw what she and Mark had away while Alexis was willing to do any and everything to get him.

It made Kim rethink her position on giving up on Mark. If a woman was willing to do this to obtain a certain man, then he must be a keeper. Once again she was torn between her two realities. This logic was quickly crushed. Before she could be swayed back to Mark, it was like an evil voice cried up from deep within her mitochondrial DNA. It was the voice of a woman scorned.

As the saying goes, hell hath no fury like a women scorned. The bare fact still remained that while Kim was at her lowest point, Mark betrayed her and strayed. While she was in the belly of Serenity fighting for her sanity, Mark was out cavorting with Alexis.

The ancient evil voice within her used this transgression to unfurl its fury. It was a fury embroiled with the trinity of lies, deception, and love. The first thing that Kim did was increase the life insurance on Mark. She continued to chase Alexis. She needed to keep up her façade. However, Alexis continued to throw shade. She captured the prize – Mark - and now she had no further use for Kim.

Kim set up one last rendezvous with Alexis. She relied on her ace in the hole. Kim now knew of Alexis's background concerning men. Kim now knew all of her history with Sam, her stepfather. She expected Alexis's reaction to her, knowing these details to be extreme.

Alexis did not disappoint. She was willing to do anything to keep Mark. Her twisted mind even prompted her to the act of murder. The threat that she felt from Kim was intense. When Kim confronted her, she swiftly decided to get rid of Kim for once and for all. Before Kim left on her mission to confront Alexis, she contacted Mark. She revealed something to him. She informed him of all of Alexis's low down ways. She told him about finding her diary and even read him the excerpts. He heard several passages that rang a bell.

"Listen, baby, I want to expose this hoe to you. I don't want Essence around this conniving bitch." Kim hoped that by playing to Mark's weakness for Essence, she could convince him. "You never know, baby," she added. "Maybe we can fix this; maybe we can get over this." Mark was reeling. "Did you know Alexis had a separate apartment?" Kim continued. "A love nest? I bet you didn't. Anyway, she agreed to meet me there. I'm going to confront her. I want you there so you can hear for yourself. You don't have to believe me. Come get it straight from the horse's mouth."

Mark considered this. That was some heavy shit that Kim laid on him. He couldn't trust it completely unless he heard it firsthand. "Alright, bet. I gots to hear this shit for myself."

Kim exhaled. Without Mark coming, there was no redemption. Kim ran down to him how they should do it. Mark was taken aback by Kim's plan. She wrapped it up. "You just stand outside the bedroom door and listen to everything. You'll be able to see what you're dealing with. Let me ask you something." Kim paused. "If I prove that she's as scandalous as I'm portraying, do you think that we can work it out?"

Mark was still thrown for a loop. "Look, Kim, I'm not making any promises. Let's just follow the plan and we'll see what's up. Just don't forget to leave the front door open." Kim wasn't interested in repairing the damage relationship. She only wanted to lure Mark in. Mark couldn't believe his ears when he was posted up outside of the bedroom door. He could hear Alexis going on as clear as day.

"I did what I had to do. Mark belongs to me now. He's mine." Her words kept ringing in his ears. Mark was befuddled at first, but after hearing Alexis out, he was too through. When he finally stepped into the bedroom to confront Alexis, he was fuming. He was ready to choke the life out of her.

"You trying to save this bitch?" he partially heard through the anger. All he could think was, *I threw everything away for this bitch. My wife, my daughter…everything.* He looked over to see Kim when he initially entered the room. Her eyes were shut tight; her lips moved silently in prayer. Seeing her cuffed to the bed caused his heart to crumble. "So you grimy like that huh, Lex?" When he glanced over at Kim again, her eyes were now open.

In her eyes were accusations mixed with guilt and on her face was a smirk. It was clearly a look that said, "This is all your fault. What are you gonna do to fix this?"

Kim's look did exactly what she knew it would. It propelled Mark into action. When Alexis swung back to Kim with the gun, Mark reacted instinctively. Before Alexis could stop herself, she pulled the trigger. There was no way she could undo what she'd set into motion.

Seeing Mark on the ground at Kim's feet was unbearable to Alexis. "She's gone, Alexis," Kim prodded. "You've killed him. He's the second man that you've killed because of your twisted take on love. First your stepfather; now Mark."

The sirens served as a type of adrenaline to Alexis. It was like she was pushed by an unseen, disagreeable source. When she scooped up the gun, Kim wasn't even on her radar. This time, Kim's voice echoed in her ears. *"He's the second man you've killed."* Alexis tried to shake her head and clear it of Kim's voice.

I can't keep going through this, Alexis reasoned. This reasoning directed her to end the saga. Without further thought, she kissed Mark. The unseen force pushed her to lay on his chest and pull the trigger.

Kim's plan came together perfectly. Once finding the diary, she wanted to punish both Mark and Alexis. For a second it was touch and go. First, she was skeptical about whether or not that Mark would come. Once he did, she knew that all would be revealed. She only hoped that she would be spared.

The upgraded insurance policy that she took out on Mark was substantial. She was set for life. There were times that she was racked with guilt and shame. Then there were times when she was at peace. Bipolar? Maybe.

In her mind, it was all fair in lies, deception, and love. She took a few wrong turns down the winding road called life, but she promised to get it straight for Essence's sake.

Little did she know that Officer Calhoun, the officer assigned to the case, wasn't totally satisfied with the outcome of the case. She sensed that everything wasn't as it seemed. Calhoun couldn't put her finger on it directly. Maybe it was female's intuition, but she vowed to keep an eye on Dr. Kimberly Stevens.

XXXXXXXXXXXXXXXXXXXXXXXXXXXX

OVA

From the author's pen...

Regardless of what one may think, there is no exact science to a perfect life. Each day that we exist above ground is a day that is or can be, affected by the choices that we make.

It is certain that we'll be held accountable for our own actions. That accountability will not only be held in the hereafter but will also be held in the here and now. Our choices, decisions, and actions can very well equate to being our life's wrong turns. Add lies, deceptions, and love to the mix, and you have the ingredients for a dramatic disaster.

No one in this universe is perfect. We've all made some wrong turns in life. The key to overcoming life's wrong turns is getting back on the right path.

Peace,

D. Shahid